CROSSING AMERICA

You Can™ Ride across The U.S. on your Motorcycle

CROSSING AMERICA

You Can™ Ride across The U.S. on your Motorcycle

Dick Peck

Q3
PRESS
Santa Rosa, California

Crossing America: You Can Ride Across the U.S. on Your Motorcycle

Published by Q3 Press, 131A Stony Circle, Suite 500, Santa Rosa, CA 95401, *www.q3press.com*

Book Design   Nancy Cutler, Midnight Oil [a design studio]

The following permissions were granted for use of selected lyrics:

Notice   The riding techniques and other suggestions made in this book are intended to help you meet the challenges of riding long distances on your motorcycle. They are in no way intended as a substitute for rider education and vigilant riding. It is strongly recommended you complete a Motorcycle Safety Foundation course, as well as regular recurrent rider training.

ISBN: 0-9724198-0-2

For Susan
Editor, venture capitalist, and friend

...I know which one of us I'd rather be.

—Hal Ketchum
The Turn of the Wheel

—

Table of Contents

Acknowledgements

A book is never just the author's work. Many people had a part in creating *Crossing America*. Here are just a few.

For encouragement, several people deserve thanks: John King, for prompting me to buy a big twin, rather than the smaller bike I chose first. Clement Salvadori, for his article, "Overcoming Inertia," which launched my first trip across the U.S. Family members on both coasts, for saying "Make the ride of your dreams," as well as for their interest and prayers as I traveled. Mary Durham (age eight at the time of this writing) for asking weekly, "What chapter are you working on now?" She kept me going.

From Michael's Harley-Davidson, three people went above and beyond the call of duty: Ron Magill, for service advice, explanations of Harley systems, and getting the bike in when the Immobilizer alarm died before my December departure. Jake Ralston, Harley-Davidson tech extraordinaire, whose knowledge, skill, and sense of craft set the standard for anyone who picks up a wrench. Walter Kettler, for good cheer, reliable information, and patient parts help from the first day I owned a Harley.

I'm also grateful to my reviewers: Michelle Ule, whose thorough edit, as well as her knowledge of California placenames, improved the book's readability and accuracy. Allan Anderson, who introduced me to the novels of Nevil Shute and read this book for its sense of story (as well as catching the final typo). Dara Leadford, whose early enthusiasm for the book and eagerness to try its advice helped determine its usefulness.

On the road, Harley-Davidson dealers helped along the way: Wyatt Wilson and the team at Harley-Davidson of Greenville, for first-rate bike prep in South Carolina prior to my SaddleSore 1,000. Harley-Davidson Buell of Tucson, for getting me in quickly to change the oil and inspect the bike, after the Indio-to-Blythe sand storm. South Valley Harley-Davidson, for their warm welcome and a great tune-up during my summer trip, when I stopped near Sandy, UT.

In Santa Rosa: John Toton and Linda Lorz, for being patient with the rider next door who believes loud pipes save lives. John Paul Scott and The Train Station, for fitness that made handling a 700-pound bike a nonevent. And friends at St. Mark Lutheran Church, whose interest was an ongoing source of support.

Very special thanks are due to the team at Q3 Press. Sharon Cauchi read the entire manuscript several times and improved both its tone and content, resulting in a much more marketable book than I wrote. Nancy Cutler designed the book cover and interior, and suggested the wonderfully appropriate "Q3" for those of us who wait until the third quarter of our lives to make some of our dreams come true.

Behind the curtain, the author's family carries a big load during the writing of most books. That has certainly been the case for *Crossing America*. My mother, Joy, has watched and worried—but also has ridden with me. She's a completely unique Q4er. In addition, she has given up family lunches, dinners, and periodically, any contact whatsoever while I was hidden away at the computer.

Finally, Susan has gone so far beyond her marital vows to bring me "good, not harm, all the days of her life," nothing I say will be adequate. She endured me wanting a bike. She bravely mounted the passenger pillion to ride down the Pacific Coast Highway and up into the Sierra. She even humors me when I say she looks great in black leather. She was the person who suggested I write about my trips. If all that weren't enough, she did the book's final edit and typeset the entire text. And through all of this, she still loves me.

Having tried to give credit where credit is due, omissions almost always occur. In the elation and exhaustion that accompany finishing a book, I'll be genuinely sorry if I missed anyone. Others made the book better than I could have alone, but the final product and any of its shortcomings are mine.

Dick Peck
Santa Rosa, CA
September 2002

Preface

You want to ride your motorcycle across the United States—or, at least, you think you do. This book is for you. In it, you'll find the whys, hows, and what to take with you on your ride. This is the book I wanted, but could not find, before I set out on my 10,000-mile journey.

On the other hand, maybe you've never thought about riding across the U.S. Perhaps you should. Motorcycle traveler and author Clement Salvadori writes, "This is your moment of opportunity, your chance to slip through the door of everyday constraints and out into the wide world. Do it! Don't even finish reading this; put on the jacket and boots and the helmet and get out there. Now! Quick!"[1]

Or, as much as you might like to go, maybe you know you just can't make a long trip right now. Your have responsibilities that must be met, or others in your family need convincing first. Read on. Beyond enjoying the ride vicariously, you can highlight (and pass along) the safety statistics—as well as some of the reasons

---

[1] Clement Salvadori, "On Touring: Overcoming Inertia," *Rider*, August 2001, p. 28.

for making rides like this. Riding your motorcycle across the U.S. is not as crazy as it seems.

The reasons why we ride, of course, are almost as varied as the bikes we choose. We ride because we like being on our motorcycles. We ride because we love being outdoors. We ride to exercise our skills. We ride because we enjoy using our bikes as transportation, whether it's to the corner store, or across state, or even across the entire country.

Yet, our reasons run deeper. We ride because we appreciate the feeling of freedom our bikes provide. We ride because we want to be alone with our thoughts. At times, we may even ride because we're unhappy at home or at work, and need the perspective that a long ride provides. Was my trip partly because I was frustrated sitting in California and doing nothing…or more accurately, seeing no results for all I was doing? Maybe so. Waiting out a recession while your industry recovers isn't fun.

So, whatever *your* reasons, this book is about riding long distances. The trips that prompted this book were a one-way 3,400-mile summer ride, with detours to see friends, across the middle of the U.S.[2]—followed by a 6,100-mile trip across the southern route and back in December.[3] But the information in this book will be helpful, even if you aren't crossing a continent. Riding 2,000 or 3,000 miles in a reasonable amount of time presents special challenges—different from local rides or leisurely touring. You'll be riding at freeway speeds, over more direct routes, and with higher daily mileage goals. How well you meet these challenges determines how enjoyable your trip will be.

---

[2] One-way from California to South Carolina, by way of Nevada, Utah, Wyoming, Colorado, Kansas, Missouri, Illinois, Indiana, Kentucky, Tennessee, and North Carolina.

[3] A roundtrip from California to South Carolina and back, crossing Arizona, New Mexico, Texas, Louisiana, Mississippi, Alabama, and Georgia.

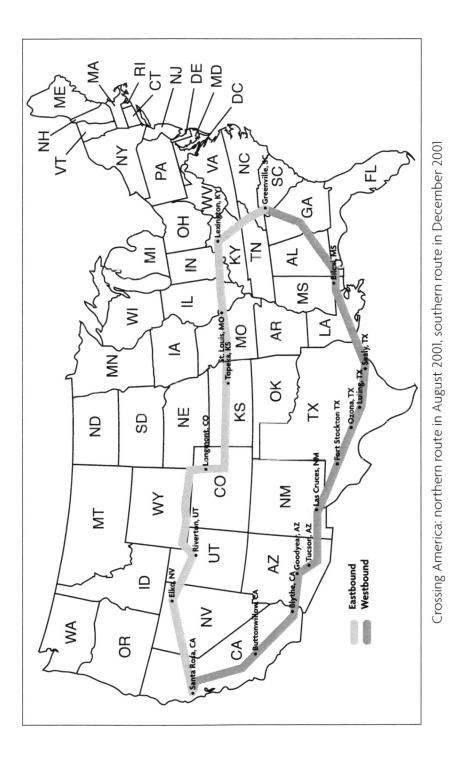

Crossing America: northern route in August 2001, southern route in December 2001

You will have more success if you tap into the experience of those who have gone before you. In addition to the information in this book, the Bibliography suggests other helpful resources.

This book also provides information on how to ship your bike home, if your schedule doesn't allow a roundtrip. On my first ride, work forced me to return home sooner than I'd hoped. Be ready, if that happens to you. And if you just don't have time to ride a complete coast-to-coast loop, don't give up on the trip. Make your first long trip a one-way ride.

Finally, beyond the whys and hows of making a long ride, this book suggests what to do to get ready and what to take. This will help you decide whether you have everything you need (or whether you are taking more than you should!). Appendix A provides a checklist of the basics you'll want to pack. Appendix B offers suggestions about what should go in your tool kit. You'll also find specific guidance in Chapter 1 about motorcycle bags and luggage. Even though your tool needs and luggage choices partly depend on your brand of bike, the general principles apply to preparing any motorcycle for a long trip. Appendix C is a supplier guide with contact information for product vendors.

I made my trip on a 1999 Harley-Davidson Softail, an FXSTB Nightrain. In certain ways, the bike we choose affects how we plan for our trips. For those who don't know Harleys, the Softail is one of Harley's "big twins." It has their largest two-cylinder engine (1,450 cc for current, fuel injected bikes; a 1,340 cc carbureted twin in mine). At 630 pounds empty, the Softail is no lightweight. On the other hand, Softails are not touring bikes like a Harley "full dresser" or BMW K1200. Harley's touring bikes tip the scales at nearly 800 pounds and come from the factory with fairings, hard bags, big tires, and softer seats.

Riding a Softail may have made my crossing more challenging than yours will be. If you're planning your trip on a Harley-Davidson

Electra Glide, a Honda Gold Wing, or a BMW K1200 LT, you may shake your head at my choice. I met riders along the way who said, "You crossed the U.S. on *that?*" On the other hand, if you're thinking about crossing America on a Ducati Monster, a Suzuki GSX-R1300 Hayabusa, or your new Buell Firebolt XB9R, have a ball—but be prepared for many more challenges than I faced by taking a non-touring bike on a long ride.

One last note: motorcycling would be poorer and we might be less inspired to ride if Clement Salvadori,[4] Ron Ayres,[5] Dave Barr,[6] Helge Pedersen,[7] Werner Bausenhart,[8] and others had not written about their travels. These riders gave me part of the encouragement I needed to get out and ride. I hope this book has the same effect for you.

Don't put off your trip any longer. Make the ride you've been promising yourself! If the book is helpful, let me know. If you find errors, point them out so they can be corrected in future editions. And if your experiences are different from mine and you think I'm off base, then tell me. Email *dick@Q3Press.com*. Good riders never stop learning.

By the way, don't be put off by the footnotes. Nothing here is difficult or academic. As a reader, I just find it more convenient to see related references on the same page as the text, not hidden at the end of the chapter or end of the book. I hope you do, too.

So, are you ready to go? Crossing America by motorcycle is a decision you'll never regret. Pour a cup of coffee or grab your favorite brew, turn the page, and let's get started.

---

[4] Clement Salvadori's article mentioned earlier—more than anything else—put me on the road.

[5] Ron Ayres, *Against the Wind: A Rider's Account of the Incredible Iron Butt Rally* (North Conway, NH: Whitehorse Press, 1997), p. 98.

[6] Dave Barr, *Riding the Edge* (Bodfish, CA: Dave Barr Publications, 1999).

[7] Helge Pedersen, *10 Years on 2 Wheels* (Seattle: Elfin Cove Press, 1998).

[8] Werner Bausenhart, *8 Around the Americas on a Motorcycle* (Brooklyn, NY: Legas, 2000).

How to Use This Book

When I began this book, I planned to call it *Crossing America by Motorcycle: Long Distances for Ordinary Riders*. But no one who crosses the United States on a motorcycle is ordinary. Any continent crossing requires a sense of adventure, good planning, decent bike handling skills, and the ability to improvise when events don't work out as you planned.

More important, every long distance rider has to have the willingness just to do the miles. Keeping your backside on the seat for 500–1,000 miles a day is no small feat. The physical conditioning and mental alertness required to complete a long distance ride successfully puts you in a special category.

You've already begun thinking about making your ride. Let's talk about how this book is organized to help you achieve that goal.

To make the book readable, but also useful for later reference, the chapters are divided into several sections, or "threads" (labeled the same way, so you can find them easily). These threads cover the topics distance riders want to know about, presented in the order you'll encounter them on your trip.

The Trip

When someone makes a long ride, we usually ask, "How did it go? What was it like?" *The Trip* section in each chapter puts us on the road together and gives you a sense of what it was like to ride across the U.S. three times in one year—one eastbound summer trip and a roundtrip during the month of December. I'll occasionally mention lessons learned from the summer trip, but focus on the December trip because winter rides require more preparation and present unique riding challenges.

Pre-Trip Preparation

After we know what a long ride is like, the next thing most of us ask is, "So, how do I get ready?" Chapter 1 is devoted to what to take, how to pack, and what to expect. For example, rain, wind, darkness, and temperature not only affect what you take—but also how you ride and what routes you choose. In subsequent chapters, the *Pre-Trip Preparation* sections add insight about things that worked well from pre-trip planning, as well as things I should have done before departing, but didn't realize until partway through the trip.

Your Equipment

The easy-to-use checklists in Appendix A and B are a starting point for what to pack and what tools to take. But that's just a start. The *Your Equipment* section of each chapter talks about how equipment choices affect you once you're on the road. How do those choices help with wind, rain, darkness, and the temperatures you'll encounter? With bike security? With dozens of other small items, from cameras to gel seat pads? *Your Equipment* offers feedback on what proved most useful during my trip (and what didn't), as well as how to get the most from your bike, your gear, and yourself along the way.

Riding Techniques

Before returning to motorcycling after a few years off, I learned to fly—earning my private pilot's license (multiengine and instrument). Pilots spend a lot of time keeping their skills current and sharing what they know with others. As riders, we need to do the same thing. *Riding Techniques* covers lane position, counter-steering, how to maintain alertness, relaxation, how to deal with crosswinds, how to combat the deadly "nanolapse," how to minimize turbulence behind trucks, and more. You're probably a good rider already or you wouldn't be reading this book. I hope you'll be an even better rider when you've finished the book.

Staying Organized

In addition to having the right equipment and good skills, nothing helps make your trip more enjoyable than staying organized. At times you'll feel overwhelmed by the number of small items needed throughout the day. Worse still, your gloves, map, wallet, keys, earplugs, and cell phone are all seeking the first possible chance to escape your care. Good carpenters say, "Measure twice, cut once." The distance rider's equivalent is "Check twice, leave once." It's no fun to return to a stop you made dozens of miles ago to retrieve an item left behind. The *Staying Organized* section appears in every other chapter throughout the book. These sections give you suggestions about pre-trip organization, as well as how to maintain order en route.

Thoughts from the Road

On long trips, we may travel farther into ourselves than over the road. Being alone with our thoughts all day gives us the opportunity to achieve, or regain, mental and emotional balance. A seagoing man once wrote (but it applies to continent-crossing riders), "exposure to physical hardship and hazard tend[s] to restore certain lost perspectives."[1] *Thoughts from the Road* recaps some of the feelings we very likely share about life and riding. But in my road ramblings, you may find new thoughts that enhance your ride—or add to your conversations with others about *why* we ride and *what we find* when we do.

Years ago the pioneers crossed America by horse and wagon train. Perhaps some of this spirit remains in us, as well. Any of us who have invested in a motorcycle and have taken a few short trips probably have a vision of setting out for points unknown with no goal but to go. Just go. Just ride.

So, let's ride together, to see if you wouldn't enjoy making the same journey.

---

[1] Ernest Gann, *Song of the Sirens* (New York: Simon and Schuster, 1968), p. 21.

Chapter 1:

There's No Place Like Home

Wednesday, December 5
Santa Rosa, CA—Mile 0

TRIP

The Trip:
Pre-Departure

Tomorrow. I'm actually leaving tomorrow. Stayed in bed late today. It's raining. It's going to be hard to leave. Part of me wants to go. Part of me wants to stay. Maybe December is not the season to cross the country on a motorcycle? Still, I'm consumed by thoughts of the upcoming trip.

Riding brings joy. There wasn't a day of my August cross-country trip that I didn't wake up happy—happy to touch my motorcycle again, excited to feel its engine come to life, joyful to lean into the first turn after an overnight stop. There wasn't a day I didn't revel in the smells of America—redwoods and clean air in Northern California; fields of grass and the soft evening air in East Kansas; smoke from roadside barbeque pits through the Deep South.

The trip was supposed to begin today, California to South Carolina and back. But I was forced to put "Eli" back into the shop on Saturday. Not everyone names their bikes, but my wife Susan christened our Softail within a week of his purchase. Just after his most recent service, however, Eli began to stumble when power

1

was rolled on. Today, the dealer found the problem: a faulty Immobilizer alarm—the only non-Harley component on the bike. The alarm was designed to completely shut down the bike when activated. But no one suspected the alarm, when the problem could have been an intake leak, fouled plugs, a timing problem, or worse.

It rained all day anyway. Rode Eli home from the dealership in the rain. Began packing, but not too successfully. Perhaps today's departure was never intended. Get a good night's sleep and then start tomorrow.

Pre-Trip Preparation: Conditioning, Route Planning, Weather

PREP

A long motorcycle trip requires planning. Yeah, we all know Larry Leatherbutt, who stuck a toothbrush in his jacket and a wallet in his pants, and rode off to find adventure. But your trip is likely to be a lot more enjoyable if you ask yourself the questions in this section.

Am I physically prepared for a long distance ride?

I regularly bike-commute 90 miles roundtrip to work. So, I ride enough under normal circumstances that getting on the bike for a 500-mile day does not produce soreness. After the first couple of days, depending on their length, I may feel fatigued—but nothing that impairs my riding ability.

How much mileage is enough to prepare adequately for a long journey?

If you can't do a local 200 miler without excessive soreness and fatigue, be sure you get into good enough physical condition to depart on a many-thousand mile journey. You don't have to be a motorcycle cop or a marathoner, but if you aren't riding enough miles, try to get regular exercise to maintain muscle tone and build reasonable endurance limits. Strength training for your upper body, abs, lower back, and legs will make the ride easier.

Is my motorcycle prepared for a long distance ride?

A mechanical problem close to home is annoying, but not a disaster. Most of us carry a cell phone and many of us have roadside assistance insurance (more about both, later). And we all know someone or someplace that services our bikes. So, the timing of a local problem may be frustrating and the expense of correcting it higher than we'd like, but we probably won't be endangered or severely inconvenienced.

The consequences of being stranded far away from home, however, can be more troublesome. You may be stuck along a desolate stretch of highway, outside cell service, and miles from the nearest repair facility. Don't ride unpopulated stretches of the Western United States without full confidence that your motorcycle is ready for the trip, particularly if you plan to ride at night. For example, Allen Bartell rode from Texas to Alaska and described his trip in the book, *Alaskan Aberration*.[1] Along the way, Bartell met a pair of riders on Honda Gold Wings who asked him to look at their tires and give an opinion whether or not they should proceed. When Bartell looked at the tires, their belts were showing through! Give the Gold Wingers credit—they were making the ride of their dreams. But try to give yourself a better chance of getting home.

Have your bike checked thoroughly by a professional who knows about the trip you are planning. Even if you're a pro, get the benefit of a second set of eyes looking at your bike's fitness. Sit with a friend and have them run through their own maintenance checklist. "Did you change…? Did you check…? Are your…OK?"

---

[1] Allen J. Bartell, *Alaskan Aberration* (Trinity, TX: Flat Black Publishing, 1997), p. 57.

Then, as a precaution, ride the bike several times before your departure. That's how Eli's alarm problem emerged. The bike had been serviced by the best Harley tech in the area. I was good to go. But pilots are taught never to go far from their home airport with an airplane that just had its annual inspection and service. Even the best airframe and power plant mechanic can be interrupted at the wrong time, forget an item you asked the shop to inspect, or miss a problem. You'll benefit by applying the same principle to your bike. Make certain to put in some miles after it's serviced, a least a week before departing on a long distance trip.

How many miles do you want to cover per day?

During my crossings, I averaged about 500 miles per day. My longest day was 1,099 miles. My shortest was 283 miles—not surprisingly, the day after I rode 1,099. How much do you want to ride daily? Your answer will vary as your trip progresses, but I'd argue that unless you average 500 miles per day, you aren't traveling—you're touring. Nothing wrong with that. It's just a different pace. For my trip, getting to my east coast destination in a week or less, and making my motorcycle a useful travel machine, was important to me. Set your daily mileage accordingly.

Where does your daily average mileage put your stops?

Pick a tentative target for the end of each day. That doesn't mean you'll actually stop there. In fact, you probably won't. For that reason, I don't recommend making reservations. Conditions change en route. But, picking a tentative stop means you have some idea about your options within 100 miles on either side of your target.

For example, let's say you were planning to ride from San Francisco to Blythe, CA, on the California-Arizona border—roughly 600 miles. Looking at a map, you would guess that lodging options beyond Blythe are limited until Phoenix, 150 miles farther. If you're determined to make Phoenix, check a motel directory or call ahead to motels between Blythe and Phoenix. On the other hand, you may not want to travel as far as Phoenix, but you do want more nightlife or amenities than you know Blythe offers. In that case, you should end your day at Palm Springs, about 100 miles west of Blythe (or only 500 miles from where you started).

What weather is forecast for your route?
Sure, you can just pack up and go. But why not get some idea what conditions will be like? Think about where you plan to be each day and check the one-, three-, and five-day forecasts. The Weather Channel is a good source of information, as are various newspapers.

However, the best sources for weather information are specialized sites on the Internet. The Weather Channel's web site, *www.weather.com*, is helpful—particularly their "Weekly Planner." Intellicast's Travel Planner is also good (*www.intellicast.com*). One of the best sites is Trucker Weather (*www.truckerweather.com*), which in addition to weather has links to each state's Department of Transportation for information about road construction and road closures.

How well-prepared are you for the forecast conditions?
Let's address your actual clothing and equipment later—key factors in being prepared. For now, think more broadly. Four conditions we face as motorcyclists are (1) wind, (2) rain, (3) darkness, and (4) outside temperature. I'm going to assume that you are not planning to ride in snow or off road, both of which present challenges beyond the purpose of this book.[2]

---

[2] If you are planning to ride in snow, sand, or mud, you may want to read both of Dave Barr's books: *Riding on the Edge* and *Riding the Ice*. You can obtain these from Dave's web site (*www.davebarr.com*) or from Whitehorse Press (*www.whitehorsepress.com*).

The effects of rain can be managed with the proper clothing and riding technique. Darkness demands that you make yourself more visible, but nighttime is manageable. And layering what you wear, adding and subtracting clothing, can buffer the outside temperature.

Wind, on the other hand, is a condition for which there are no good mitigating strategies. Other than adding a windscreen or fairings, dealing with wind is entirely a matter of technique—lean angle and throttle control. You simply ride it out. So pay attention to the forecasts along your route for windy conditions. You'll have to ride with more caution. You may need to reduce speed. In some cases (for example, during dust and sand storms in desert areas), you simply may decide to sit it out until conditions change.

EQUIP

Your Equipment:
Packing List, Tool Kit, Luggage

A big part of making a long distance trip is deciding what to take and how to carry it. You must decide (1) what is essential to *your* comfort and safety and (2) how much you can comfortably carry—and then how to strike a deal between (1) and (2) when you begin loading your bike.

Packing and tool kit checklists

Appendix A provides a packing checklist, while Appendix B details what I carried in my tool kit. I compiled these lists by emptying my bags after the trip and inventorying every item. Look over the lists in these two appendixes as you prepare. For your ride, what I carried may be too much. For other rides, it will be too little. Appendix B includes a blank form for you to add your own items.

Look at packing and tool kit checklists available in other publications and on the Internet, as well. For example, I patterned my tool kit for the Softail after the suggestions in *How to Set Up*

Your Motorcycle Workshop, by C.G. Masi.[3] You may also want to have a look at *www.ironbutt.com* and click "Archive of Wisdom." Then look for the link to "Ron Major's Tool Kit," under Tip 21. Compare those two with mine, in Appendix B. Both exceed what I carried, but my mechanical skills are pretty basic. Think, too, about any brand- or model-specific items you ought to carry. If you're riding something exotic, you can be sure you aren't going to find parts in many of the places along your route.

In the end, you are the best judge of what *you* need. Just be sure to lay it all out beside your bike and do a "trial packing" before the day of departure. Most of us make some final compromises as we stand beside our bikes, comparing what we think we need to the space available. Be sure you do this no later than the night before you depart. Making the necessary compromises took me longer than I thought it would and contributed to a delayed start. Start early. Make a pre-trip checklist. Try putting it all in your bike luggage. You'll thank yourself when departure day comes. As an added benefit, you have your list ready for trips number two, three, and beyond!

Luggage

Believe it or not, one of the most important factors affecting your trip, after your physical condition and the reliability of your bike, is your bike's luggage. Why? Because you are going to use your bags several times a day. You will also tote some or all of the bags' content into your room or tent every night. The longer your trip, the more you'll appreciate good bags.

If you're riding a factory-designed tourer, congratulations. But many bikes do not come with factory-supplied bags, and riders

---

[3] C.G. Masi, *How to Set Up Your Motorcycle Workshop* (North Conway, NH: Whitehorse Press, 1996). See especially Chapter 10, "The Emergency Tool Kit."

have to start from scratch choosing luggage. Even if your bike came with factory-supplied bags or a hard "trunk," you still probably need to add at least a couple of soft bags or bungee some extra items on a rack. If so, the discussion that follows should help.

First, be sure your luggage passes the U.S. Post Office motto test. You know, "Neither rain, nor sleet, nor hail shall keep us from our appointed rounds." For the distance rider, it's more like "Neither road speeds, nor wind, nor significant bumps shall keep your luggage from reaching its appointed destination." Make sure your luggage attaches securely.

Sounds simple, doesn't it? It's not. My wife and I once made a short trip down the Pacific Coast Highway and back. On that trip, we rode with a group. A few miles below San Francisco, my sleeping bag—which we had firmly anchored to the sissy bar with bungee cords—squirted out from its place between two other nylon stuff sacks. Thankfully, our loss was only embarrassing. A rider behind us saw the bag leave our bike. He turned around, retrieved the bag, and handed it to us at the next stop. But we would have lost it completely, had we not been in a group.

Losing a bag could also result in a dangerous situation. A large object falling from your bike might cause someone behind to swerve into traffic. On the other hand, if the object only partially falls from your bike, you may be the one at risk. The danger comes from retaining straps, bungee cords, or the object itself falling into your running gear. Another rider on that same trip told us of having once lost a tent. The airflow behind his bike sucked the tent out of its stuff sack. The turbulence behind the bike then flipped part of the tent into his rear sprocket and locked the rear wheel. He emerged unhurt, but in other circumstances or heavy traffic, that might not have been the case.

Second, make certain the weight and location of your luggage doesn't affect the handling of your bike. We'll return to the importance of motorcycle weight and balance in the "Riding Techniques" section of this chapter. For now, just be sure you choose your luggage with its overall weight, placement, and effects on handling, in mind.

Third, don't forget you're going to handle your luggage several times a day. When you stop in the evening, you'll take at least some items into your motel or tent. Do you take those items out of your bags? Or do you remove the bags? How hard will that be? Do you plan to remove *all* your luggage from the bike every night? Or can you put what you need in easy-to-remove pieces and protect whatever you leave on the bike?

Moreover, you won't use your luggage just at night. As you ride, weather conditions change. Mornings will be cooler than afternoons. Rain will start and stop. You'll start out the day wearing clothes that you'll later want to stow.

Think about this as you choose your luggage or decide how to use what came on your bike. Where do you put your jacket when the day warms up? How long does that take? Where do you keep your rain suit, gaiters, and other wet weather gear? Where do you put smaller items like a second pair of gloves, your sunglasses, or a bottle of drinking water? What else do you need to carry that you cannot, or do not want to, keep in your jacket? Your wallet? Keys to your motorcycle? A small camera? Bills and change for refreshment stops and tolls?

I strongly suggest you follow two rules for successful luggage handling:

Rule Number One: Outside Pockets

Make sure your luggage has enough outside pockets to hold the items you want available throughout the day. On my winter trip I kept my lightweight gloves and a Polartec ski cap just inside a zipper pocket I could reach quickly. Other items for outside pockets include a flashlight, maps, wallet, keys, earplugs, cell phone, and pocket change.

Rule Number Two: Free Space

Don't start your trip with your luggage full. Leave as much as 20% of the space free. You're going to need a place to put your jacket, or to swap your jacket for raingear when the weather changes. Plus, regardless of how well you pack, things won't fit into your luggage as neatly on the road as they do at home. The first time you unpack, and then try to put everything back where it was, you'll either spend more time than necessary or you'll find stuff no longer fits—maybe both! Leave space in your luggage for later. I promise, you'll thank me.

Finally, think about how to handle your bike and your gear during nightly stops. If you cannot leave part of your luggage on the bike overnight, you're going to have to transport your bags (or their contents) from the bike to your lodging every night. If your room is across a parking lot, through the lobby, up an elevator or stairs, and down a long hallway, how many trips do you want to make? You'll quickly decide, "One!"

Luggage checklist

Use the checklist on the following page to evaluate your current bike bags or to help you purchase new motorcycle luggage. Appendix C lists supplier information.

Luggage Checklist

❏ Are the bags designed for your bike? If not, do they mount securely and in locations that don't create weight and balance problems?

❏ Do the bags attach and detach conveniently—or will you grow to despise wrestling with them every night? You don't want to fight a tangle of bungee cords after riding 500 or more miles!

❏ If your bike came equipped with hard bags, do they have liners you can remove to carry your gear into your lodging? If not, you may want to pack items in heavy duty trash bags or bring along a couple of canvas totes.

❏ Does the capacity meet your needs, without making your luggage too heavy for the bike or to carry into your room or tent every night?

❏ If you have multiple pieces, do they attach securely to each other—or securely to the bike, in convenient locations?

❏ Is some part of the luggage waterproof? Remember, not every part needs to resist rain. Your bike cover, tent, and raingear won't be affected by rain.

❏ Does your luggage have enough small pockets and easily accessible places for the items you need as you ride?

❏ Do you have a good shoulder strap, to assist with carrying your luggage to your lodging each night? If not, see the recommendation in Appendix A.

❏ Does your luggage have D-rings or other attachment points for the strap?

❏ When you look at the carrying capacity on your bike, are you comfortable? You're going to have to live with your choice for hundreds or thousands of miles. Don't leave home until you are satisfied!

My luggage choices

What did I use? For saddlebags, I chose LeatherLyke Cross Country Bags—Model 225, the big ones, rather than their smaller cruiser bags.[4] These are hard bags, manufactured to look like leather, with hinged tops and locks. I packed the left-hand bag exclusively with items I would not need until my destination. My hard bags stayed on the bike every night.

For bulkier items (second helmet, raingear, bike cover, and so on), I used a two-bag combination of nylon luggage—The SAC and Cool SAC, by Elmwood Specialty Products. The larger bag, The SAC, rests on the luggage rack over the rear fender. It has a pocket that fits over the Softail's sissy bar pad, along with webbed straps to secure the bag to the bar itself. The Cool SAC is smaller and connects to the larger bag with D-rings. This bag also has straps for using it alone, which was a handy benefit for day trips at my destination. Zippers on both bags allow quick access to add and remove items. The figure below shows how the bags work together.

Softail with all luggage in place

---

[4] See Appendix C, "Supplier Directory," for company contact information.

The larger bag is not waterproof. Anything that needed to stay dry, I packed in trash bags. The smaller bag has a removable vinyl liner. I used the liner to keep rain out and packed it with my toiletries kit and extra underwear. But on a hot, midsummer afternoon in Nevada, I'd put my gear elsewhere, fill the liner with ice, and carry my beverage of choice!

Finally, my nomination for the most useful luggage of the trip is Don Hood's Lazy Rider bag.[5] You need to own a cruiser-style bike with a sissy bar to use Don's product. But if that describes your machine, the Lazy Rider bag serves as luggage *and* an adjustable rider backrest, with lumbar support. I bought the 12-inch diameter bag. It fits my Softail perfectly, makes riding long distances more comfortable, and holds an amazing amount of gear. It also provided an anchor-point for the Cool SAC's straps, so all three bags became a single unit anchored to each other from opposite sides of the sissy bar. This assembly easily passed the Post Office motto test!

Riding Techniques: Loads and Handling

RIDE

A loaded bike won't handle like an empty bike with a solo rider. That's obvious. A bike loaded with luggage is not only more sluggish, but may also be dangerous—if you don't pay attention to the placement and weight of your luggage.

The capacity rating of your tires affects the amount of weight you can carry. What is the total weight your bike's tires are capable of supporting? Your owner's manual should include a maximum figure. If you swapped the original tires for a different size or type, of course, you'll need to do the arithmetic yourself. Remember that the total supported by the tires must include the empty weight of

---

[5]See *www.lazyrider.com* for more information.

the bike, all fluids (figure an average of seven pounds per gallon for gas and oil), the rider(s), and all luggage, including its contents.

How much you put in each piece of luggage matters, too. For example, hard saddlebags often have a sticker inside stating the maximum weight they can carry safely. If you've added a luggage rack, you probably saw the warnings—either stickered on the rack or shown in accompanying product information—stating the carrying capacity of the rack. Heed those warnings.

Finally, where you mount your luggage matters, too. Keep the weight as low as possible to keep the bike's center of gravity low, for stability. For example, if you purchased a fairly tall sissy bar bag, put heavy items in the bottom, not near the top. Also, keep as much weight as possible between the axles. Weight hanging off the back of the bike could make its steering light. You don't want to discover this in an uphill, decreasing radius turn along the Pacific Coast Highway. Weight above or beyond the front axle increases steering effort, makes the bike less responsive, and causes it to "plow" into turns. Load your bike in a way that maintains its original handling, so far as possible.

Staying Organized: Small Items and Bagging Your Clothes

Once you've decided on a luggage system, be consistent about where you put your stuff en route so you always know where things are. You may find that an additional bag or two inside your luggage makes corralling small items easier. In my right-hand hard saddlebag, I kept an old canvas shoulder bag, or messenger bag, purchased years ago at a college bookstore. This bag's function was to organize the small items so they were accessible throughout the day. The bag is shaped so that it slips inside my saddlebag. In addition, it has lots of zippered pockets and can be thrown over a shoulder allowing me to grab quickly everything I needed for a gas, food, or rest stop. You may want to find a similar bag.

Packing the contents of your larger luggage in plastic bags does more than protect contents against the weather. Bagging items also helps keep things organized along the way. Wastebasket-sized trash bags, along with gallon- and sandwich-sized Ziploc bags, are all useful. Use these informal organizers to make daily packing and unpacking easier. Not only does the contents of your luggage stay better organized, but the plastic bags help things slide in and out of your luggage more quickly than trying to pack jeans, T-shirts, and underwear in the conventional way.

Thoughts from the Road: Why Do We Ride?

The trip begins tomorrow. My alarm is set. Bags are packed. Better weather is forecast. I'm looking forward to the ride. But is that why I'm going? A friend asked, "Why are you *really* doing this?"

Why, indeed? We seldom ride *only* to get somewhere. One reason for this journey is to complete my unfinished summer trip. After riding from California to South Carolina, I had to fly home and ship the bike back. The result was a sense of unfinished business, riding business; a challenge unmet. But was that the only reason? Why do we really ride?

"Good highways afford great opportunity for flights of thought," Werner Bausenhart wrote.[6] You are alone with your thoughts, mile upon mile, hour after hour.

You also have a chance to break out of your normal routine. Scientist Mitchell Feigenbaum attempted the ultimate break from routine. Finding a 24-hour day too confining, Feigenbaum

---

[6] Bausenhart, *Around the Americas*, p. 149.

experimented with 26-hour days. This resulted in his schedule swinging in and out of phase with colleagues working more normal schedules at Los Alamos National Laboratory.[7] Often, Feigenbaum would spend hours at nights, walking in the dark— thinking. My route would pass closer to Las Cruces, NM, than Los Alamos. Maybe that's a good thing. I'd rather be on a bike than walking in the deserts in the dark.

But *why* does time to think make some people so uncomfortable? Is it because we don't really like what we see inside ourselves? Or is it because we don't find *anything* inside, like empty clouds that drop no rain? Surely there aren't people who have no interests; nothing that excites them; nothing to think about, ponder, or argue with themselves. Are we uncomfortable with ourselves because we lack imagination?

Or do we fear failure? Fear trying what we haven't previously attempted? T.S. Eliot wrote, "Only those who risk going too far can possibly find out how far they can go."[8] This trip will not fully explore how far I can go, but it will stretch me beyond previous limits.

Why *am* I doing this?

Ride. Get out of town and ride. Just ride.

---

[7] James Gleick, *Chaos: Making a New Science* (New York: Viking Penguin, Inc., 1987), pp. 1-2.

[8] Quoted on a *Runner's World* screen saver, downloadable from *www.runnersworld.com*.

Chapter 2:

Beginnings
Thursday, December 6
Santa Rosa, CA to Buttonwillow, CA—324 miles

The Trip:
California's Central Valley

Seconds before noon, Eli's engine fires solidly. His ignition difficulties seem to have been solved. My dog, Dudley, barks. He is never happy when I leave. He knows the sound of Eli's pipes and is always standing at the window when I return. He'll have to wait a bit longer than usual this time.

Leaving at noon was hardly deliberate. But I didn't finish packing the bike last night, as I should have. Don't know if it was the rain or my doubts that held me back. Today, just suiting up was a challenge. It felt like dressing to fly the space shuttle, although I looked more like a kid about to go out and play in the snow. In August, a couple of layers had provided plenty of warmth. Mornings were cool, but by midday my jacket went on the sissy bar and I could ride in a T-shirt and jeans. Not so, this trip. I'm wearing wool tights under leather jeans, with chaps over the jeans. On top, I have on a T-shirt, cotton turtleneck, and electric jacket liner in addition to my leather jacket.

Sometimes I think about fancy Cordura nylon outerwear. But my children gave me this jacket when I bought the bike. It was made by San Diego Leathers, the same place I bought my first pilot's jacket. This jacket and I have seen some good miles together. You don't give up on family, or a faithful jacket, lightly.

Departure from Santa Rosa

With a glance over my shoulder, a wave to Susan and my mom, the trip has begun. Riding slowly through beautiful countryside, I wend my way across Sonoma County, then through Napa, toward I-5 south. Traffic moves smoothly once past a minor fender-bender on Highway 121, the Carneros Highway. The Carneros spans the bottom of Sonoma and Napa counties. Its rolling hills are great for wine grapes that like cool weather. Morning fog and the breezes off San Pablo Bay guard the pinot noir and chardonnay through which I'm riding.

At 167 miles, I make my first stop in Santa Nella along I-5. The sun is warm now. Bakersfield is the goal today, only 330 miles—a short day because of my late departure. Stopping the bike at my first mini-mart of the trip, I get gas and take off my jacket briefly to eat a quick snack. The morning fog was chilly in Sonoma and Napa counties. It would be wonderful just to bask in the sun here for a while. But that won't get me to Bakersfield before dark. My late start has put me behind the original goal for today—which was to go as far as Blythe, on the California-Arizona border.

Back on I-5, the broad expanse of California's central valley continues to roll by. This valley, stretching roughly from Redding to Bakersfield is California's "bread belt," the source of much of California's food and the nation's. Some 450 miles long north to south, the central valley would stretch from Chicago to Pittsburgh. Forty to sixty miles wide, the valley includes eighteen counties and five million people—one-sixth of California's population.[1]

Vast farms tended by large agricultural operations occupy this sometimes-overlooked area. The glitz of Hollywood and the wacky politics of San Francisco and the Bay Area overshadow a lot of hard working folks, living straightforward lives, on this land that comprises two-fifths of the area of the state. It's pleasant today, riding through its wide-open spaces and deep blue skies. Already, I begin to wish for more time than I have available for my trip.

Traffic is heavier than I expected, mid-day and mid-week. Still, the vehicles around me have settled into a relaxed pace right at the speed limit. I'm able to enjoy the warm air and savor the fact I'm on the road again. Except for road construction on I-5 just north of Bakersfield, I'd have arrived at Buttonwillow, just outside Bakersfield before dark. As I pull off I-5 and into the Super 8, the front desk staff is putting up a Christmas tree in the lobby. Seeing the tree renews the tension between "wanna go" and "wanna stay." I've undertaken this trip at one of the strangest possible times—in the middle of winter and during the month when most folks spend

---

[1] For more about this wonderful part of the state, see *www.library.ca.gov/CRB/97/09/#Heading1*.

evenings shopping for gifts and enjoying time with family and good friends.

But I've begun. The trip is actually underway. That's the first step. My average speed was above 60 miles per hour today and the 300 miles were safe. Walk to dinner at Willow Ranch, a barbeque restaurant across from the motel, next to a T/A truck stop. The restaurant is full, but I find a table. Even the local CHP, the California Highway Patrol, are there on a dinner break. The restaurant makes good barbeque, enjoyed with a Sierra Nevada Pale Ale. At a mini-mart on the walk back to the motel, I buy cottage cheese to eat for breakfast tomorrow. Sometimes getting started is the hardest part of any task, even a pleasurable one. But, I did start, and Day One is complete.

PREP

Pre-Trip Preparation: Heated Clothing

If you're thinking about a winter trip—but have never used electric clothing—don't leave home without it. American Express may say the same thing about their charge card, but you are going to appreciate your electric clothing a lot more!

I looked at various types of heated clothing, read the tests,[2] and picked Gerbing's. The reasons? First, Jeff Gerbing was wonderful about answering email. He patiently responded to all my questions. Second, Gerbing makes the Harley-branded electric clothing. My choice was not based on needing a Harley label, but rather, wanting to be sure nothing affected Eli's extended warranty.

---

[2] One such test can be found at *www.motorsports-network.com/prodtest.HTM*. Always check for the most recent information, however. Note, too, that there has been some controversy about the testing methodology. Widder, particularly, objected to one widely published test on the basis that the method used didn't fairly measure heat output. As always, if you can find friends who own the type of gear you are considering (or if you find an online question and answer forum), real world endorsements are the best way to confirm a manufacturer's claims and test results.

Electric clothing garment tag with requirements

A bike's alternator puts out a certain amount of current. That current is used to run any electrical gear on the motorcycle, as well as to charge its battery. Electric clothing draws current (amperage) directly from the battery. If you exceed the alternator's output with your clothing, the battery will gradually discharge, instead of charging, while you ride. If Eli's battery suddenly began to discharge, or a problem arose with the alternator, I wanted a garment information tag that made it clear Harley had reviewed that particular garment's amperage requirements and agreed the alternator's output was adequate.

You should be sure you know the same for your bike—that is, how much output can your clothing require before risking battery discharge? Harley's garment tags show all possible combinations of vests, jacket liners, gloves, pants, and even socks. For the most common combinations, the tag shows total amps drawn and the RPM at which the bike must run to provide enough alternator output. If you don't ride a Harley or choose not to purchase Gerbing's Harley-branded clothing, be sure you know the same information your bike/clothing combination.

As you look at heated clothing, don't be put off by the variety of choices. You'll find electric vests versus complete jacket liners. You'll find some manufacturers offer separate sleeves and detachable collars. Others don't. Then, there are the gloves, pants, and even socks to consider.

My recommendations? If your bike doesn't have heated handgrips, get electric gloves. Second, get a full jacket liner, not just a vest. You don't want cold arms between your heated vest and heated gloves. With a jacket liner and gloves, you will be amazingly warm, even without heated clothing for the lower half of your body. One company explains it this way: if your torso is warm, it signals the rest of your body that there's no need for alarm, plenty of heat is available. And as odd as that sounds, it works—even at 75 mph road speeds and temperatures as low as 28 degrees. Only once during the trip did I think about heated socks. Even then, if I had put on rain gaiters over my boots, I think I'd have been sufficiently warm again.

Try on several types of gloves before making a purchase, if possible. Fit and flexibility are important when riding eight or more hours daily. So is water protection. I haven't yet found a perfect balance of these—fit, flexibility, and water protection. Electric gloves are designed to protect you against the cold, so they're generally heavy. Heavy equals stiff. Stiff makes it harder to manipulate controls, turn signals, and zippers. Stiff can also cause seams or a bend in the leather at an awkward place, to create a blister after hundreds of miles. During this trip, I ended up with a blister on each hand—not a big deal on a trip of more than 6,000 miles, but annoying. On the other hand, the Gerbing gloves stood up well to two rainy days. My hands were damp but not drenched.

In an email shortly before departure, Jeff had assured me there was no danger of electrical shock. I took him at his word. He was right.

EQUIP

Your Equipment:
Phones, Motorcycle Seats, and Navigation Gear

If you're making a summer trip, you probably won't need electric clothing in most locations. But the chances are good at any time of year (1) you'll need to call home or call ahead, (2) you'll want a comfortable place to sit, and (3) you'd like to know you're on the right road and where the next turn comes.

Cell phones

Let's start with the simplest item—a cellular phone. Most of own cell phones today. If you haven't purchased one yet, I strongly recommend getting one for your trip. It doesn't have to have email, a web browser, and the ability to play a dozen different tunes. The cheapest phone that allows you to make calls from the road will add greatly to your peace of mind and safety. A nationwide calling plan may cost a bit more each month, but the savings in long distance and roaming charges more than make up the difference.

With a cell phone and a road service membership,[3] you should never be stuck—unless you are out of range of a cell tower. Some riders also equip their touring motorcycles with citizen's band, or CB, radios. While this might help in the most unpopulated stretches out West, you're equally likely to have a passing motorist or trucker stop to help.

In addition to breakdown protection, your cell phone allows you to make calls almost anywhere you stop, rather than having

---

[3] Try Road America out of Coral Gables, FL. Call them at 1 888 443-5896 or check online at *www.road-america.com/ca/hd/Enrollment.html*. If you don't own a Harley-Davidson or a Buell, check with your dealer to see who provides emergency road service for your brand. Note, however, that most automobile roadside assistance programs do not include motorcycle service.

to find a pay phone. The time saved, the ability to stay in touch
with family and friends (even other riders on the same trip), and
the security in being able to call for help *all* make carrying a cell
phone worthwhile.

Seats

You'll hear a lot of theories about how to take the load off your
sensitive parts. Part of the answer, of course, is to ride regularly. As
discussed in Chapter 1, if you aren't in shape to ride, the first few
days of your trip may prove more painful than satisfying. You don't
have to be Arnold Schwarzenegger, but you do have to build a
sufficient mileage base so your backside doesn't begin to protest
within 100 miles of home.

Despite that, even the best-prepared rider can get a "hot spot."
So, for example, don't carry your wallet in a rear pocket. The
flatter and smoother you make the contact between your buns and
the seat, the better the ride's gonna be.

Another part of riding comfortably is your motorcycle seat
itself. If you look at the skinny seats on racing bicycles in the Tour
de France, you'll know we motorcyclists have nothing to complain
about. On the other hand, some motorcycle seats are better than
others for a long trip.

Harley's Nightrain model ships from the factory with a "bar bike"
seat. You probably know the type. They're streamlined, shaped
to emphasize the lines of the frame, from fuel tank to rear fender.
They're thin, to enhance that line. And they taper rapidly, leaving
little if any cushion for a passenger. Eli, a Nightrain, left Harley's
York, PA, Final Assembly plant with such a seat. However, Eli
arrived in our garage with a Softail Custom seat—a more
conventional two-up seat, including a sissy bar and backrest.

That said, the plushest-appearing seat might not be best. Do
the edges catch your legs at an awkward spot? Susan has this

problem with Eli's current passenger pillion. Yet a wider seat is not always better. The wider pillion on a Heritage Softail we rented for the Milwaukee 2000 Annual Rally proved even more uncomfortable for her. The same can prove true for the rider.

Susan contemplating Eli's seat (on a short trip to Reno)

The firmness of the padding is also a factor. For the same reason bedding manufacturers offer soft, firm, and extra-firm mattresses, motorcycle seats come with different degrees of firmness. Unlike mattresses, however, seats are not usually labeled, so you need to try them out. Some riders prefer to sink down into the seat. Others are comfortable only on more firmly padded seats. And some riders are sold on aftermarket gel-padded seats.[4]

---

[4] Accessory strap-on gel pads, particularly, seem to prove annoying for most people—difficult to keep in place and providing little added comfort. One rider I know finally gave up and just threw a sheepskin over his seat. If you try this, just be sure the sheepskin doesn't hang over the engine or fall into your bike's drive train.

The choice is yours. A softer seat will compress over time and require replacement, depending on your weight and how many miles you ride. Eli's foam-padded seat is on the softer side. But I weigh 190 lbs and have gotten almost 25,000 miles from the current seat. Only now am I beginning to feel any compression or loss of resilience. Occasionally a rider will talk of getting 10,000 miles or less from a seat, but this is rare.

Another factor is the base-plate—the form on which the seat padding is mounted. Some Harley riders believe factory seats are easier on the backside because their base-plates are flexible. Other riders swear by steel base plates. The bottom line? I'm convinced that comfort depends first on the miles you've ridden to prepare, and second, on your fanny's match with the seat. Added padding may help. The base-plate may make a difference. But if you haven't taught your backside to sit for hours, don't waste money swapping seats or purchasing extra, strap-on gel pads.

One final thought: some aftermarket seat makers suggest break-in periods of as much as 1,000 miles for new seats. This is often true of leather (rather than vinyl), with firm padding. My approach to motorcycle seats is the same as running shoes or hiking boots. No break-in should be necessary with modern materials and design. Either way, however, find a dealer who will allow you to mount the seat you are considering on your bike. Better yet, take it for a short ride, if they'll let you. Best of all, get a promise you can return the seat for an exchange or refund, if necessary. In any case, don't leave home for a long journey without a seat you have tested and proven for at least a few hundred miles.

Navigation gear

Even America's most heavily traveled roads—the interstate highways—are not always well marked. To make sure you're on the right road for you destination, you need navigation gear.

Maps and atlases.   At a minimum, be sure you have the simplest navigation tool: a good atlas or a set of maps for the states you plan to cross. I carried the Harley Owners Group (HOG) atlas, because it was more compact than most atlases and included a complete list of dealers. The dealership list turned out to be handy when I encountered an unexpected sand storm near the Arizona-California border and wanted Eli's oil changed before continuing.

Auto clubs often provide customized mapping services. If you already belong, stop by an office or phone your club with trip details. If you aren't a member, you should check out AAA's Internet TripTik service. Go to the Association's web site[5] and under "Travel," click Internet TripTik. You'll be asked to register, but registration is free. You can enter your point of origin, your destination address, and up to 10 waypoints in between, for a total of 12 points. AAA's computers create custom maps, provide written directions, and even mark possible road construction and delays.

Mapping software and Internet maps.   You may prefer electronic maps to paper. The Internet offers a wealth of mapping sites, which didn't exist as little as a decade ago. Two good places to start are MapQuest[6] and Yahoo! Maps.[7] I find the user interface for Yahoo! Maps a little easier, while Susan is a confirmed MapQuest user. And, MapQuest's Road Trip Planner feature offers many of the features of AAA's TripTik. However, like TripTik, Road Trip Planner imposes a waypoint limit—10 points, including the point from which you started.

If MapQuest, Yahoo Maps, and the Internet TripTik don't satisfy you, you may be a candidate for mapping software. Programs

---

[5] In California, I consulted the California State Automobile Association at *www.csaa.com*. The umbrella site for AAA is *www.aaa.com*.

[6] See *www.mapquest.com*.

[7] See *maps.yahoo.com*.

like *Street Atlas USA*[8] and *Street Wizard*[9] have become popular alternatives for travel planning. Just be aware that the program and data files can be quite large. This sort of software is better suited for newer computers. Check the software company's system recommendations carefully.

One interesting feature of many mapping software products is their ability to link to a GPS system (see the following section). If you know you plan to use a GPS to navigate on your trip, be sure it is compatible with the mapping software you choose.

Global positioning system (GPS). Before beginning this section, I should make my motorcycling prejudices clear. Although I want all the information available when flying an airplane, my preference on a bike is to keep the experience as simple and pure as possible. A GPS with a moving map is incredibly helpful while flying in the clouds. It fills an information *void* that keeps pilots safe.

In our daily lives, however, most of us face information *overload*. At home and at work, newspapers, email, magazines, TV, the Web, and stacks of paperwork confront us. As a result, getting on a bike is a way of regaining the perspective lost to a life out of control. For that reason, I don't use a GPS on my bike.

Having admitted that, when I rode my SaddleSore 1,000 (see Chapter 9), I would have welcomed the help a GPS can provide. And my wife would have welcomed not being kept awake during the night, by my calls asking her to double-check on the Web how far I'd traveled. So, make your own decision about the type of riding you intend to do and the usefulness of GPS for your purposes.

---

[8] See *www.delorme.co*. However, *Street Atlas 2003* would not install properly on my Windows NT machine and I spent 17 minutes holding for tech support before they disconnected me. It did install under Windows 2000, but the interface was non-intuitive and did not use standard Windows interface conventions. Also, the software did not include printed documentation.

[9] See *www.streetwizard.com*.

In simple terms, GPS technology relies on a vehicle-mounted unit that receives position information from special satellites orbiting the earth. By triangulating your position (that is, by three or more satellites in different locations automatically locating and confirming where you are), the GPS unit displays your vehicle's location on a moving map, along with information about speed, distances, and progress toward your destination. Most GPS units even recalculate your route if you make a detour or a side trip, suggesting directions from your location when the side trip is complete.

Such convenience comes at a price. The unit I recommend, the Garmin StreetPilot III Deluxe, sells for about $700-800 through electronics discounters.[10] The display on these units is extraordinary. Clear color and fine detail is easily visible in bright sunlight. Much of this technology was developed for boating and aviation units, which are even more expensive, so motorists and bike riders benefit with good technology and cheaper prices. For example, a roughly equivalent Garmin aviation GPS unit, the GPSMAP 295, sells for $1,449.00.

The biggest drawback to the StreetPilot is the map source information comes on a CD ROM. One region is provided when you purchase your GPS. However, to cross America you need information from four—possibly more—regions depending on your route. You also need a computer to upload the data to the GPS. Before deciding that GPS is the way to go, be certain you are prepared to bring along the additional technology required.

If technology is no barrier, the biggest problem with using GPS is that you may end up having so much fun with the unit, you forget to pay attention to your riding! Use GPS with care. Like anything that slows down your scan (see the next section, "Riding

---

[10] See *www.gpscity.com/products/garmin/streetpilotiii.html,* which at the time of writing offered the StreetPilot III at roughly $700 and the StreetPilot III Deluxe at about $800.

Techniques: S.I.P.D.E."), too much attention to your GPS could have serious consequences.

Some of the top manufacturers of handheld and motorcycle-suitable GPS units include Garmin, Magellan, and Lowrance. Specialist companies such as Trimble, UPS Aviation Technologies, Honeywell/Bendix King, Furuno, Raytheon, and others make systems for aviation and marine applications.

Information about GPS changes so quickly—just like personal computers and software—it would be pointless to include specific comparisons here. The information would almost certainly be out of date by the time you read it. Instead, check the web sites listed in the footnote on this page or do a Web search using Google (*www.google.com*) to search for GPS-related sites. Be sure you have the most current information.[11]

 Riding Techniques: S.I.P.D.E.

RIDE On the way today, the mental discipline of riding at road speeds returned quickly. Anyone who has ridden a motorcycle knows that vigilance is the rider's best friend.

The Motorcycle Safety Foundation (MSF)[12] teaches SIPDE:

*S*can, *I*dentify, *P*redict, *D*ecide, *E*xecute

P also can be expanded to stand for "predict and parse," since multiple threats often exist. Divide or parse the threats whenever

---

[11] Two excellent sites are *http://joe.mehaffey.com/ot-20.htm*, which provides a comparison of several manufacturer's handheld GPS units, updated as recently as June 2002, and also *www.cycoactive.com/gps/default.htm*, which provides an excellent comparison of the Garmin units. The Cycoactive site also warns about some pitfalls you need to be aware of, such as the effect of vibration and how to mount your GPS. Even BMW, who offer wonderful dash-mounted GPS units in their automobiles, still use the equivalent of externally-mounted handhelds for motorcycle applications.

[12] See *www.msf-usa.org* for more information about MSF programs and training.

possible. Minimizing one danger—by allowing a car to pass on your left, for example—provides more time to pay attention to others (the car about to emerge from an intersection to your right, for example). Keith Code teaches superbike racers to imagine that they have $10 worth of attention.[13] The key to staying safe is being aware of how that $10 is spent. If you are spending $9 worth of attention to be sure the car on your right doesn't pull out in front of you, you only have $1 worth of attention for what's happening on your left.

The most important of all SIPDE's actions is *scan*. Riding a motorcycle in traffic is a little bit like flying an airplane using only instruments. As you fly in the clouds, you repeatedly scan your instruments to ensure that your aircraft is level and on course. On a motorcycle, however, instead of instruments, you scan:

- Traffic to the *front*
- Traffic in your *mirrors*
- Traffic and any other hazards to your *sides*

Obviously, what happens ahead is important. But whoever is approaching from behind can be almost as important. After riding a while, you get a sense of which drivers behind you are dangerous. They approach too fast. They follow too closely. Your motorcycle represents a challenge to them. Their behavior says they feel you shouldn't be on the road at all and certainly should not be in front of them. Drivers like this communicate their anger in subtle and not-so-subtle ways. Scan your mirrors regularly to find them, before they become a threat, by scanning regularly. Let 'em pass. You

---

[13] Keith Code, *A Twist of the Wrist* (Glendale, CA: Code Break, 1997), p. xii. Keith runs The Superbike School (*www.superbikeschool.com*). While the course is taught on road racing tracks, his two books, *A Twist of the Wrist* Volume 1 and Volume 2, are useful even if you never plan to race, because they teach you to think.

learn humility on a motorcycle. Maybe the world would be a better place if more people rode bikes.

Your scan includes more than traffic, however. Use your peripheral vision to scan pavement conditions, as well as movement along the shoulder, which could be a dog or a deer. You should even include your bike in your scan. After losing our sleeping bag on the coast trip mentioned in Chapter 1, my peripheral scan now includes luggage. I load the bike so in my mirrors I can see everything that might shift or work loose. Riding today, for example, I was able to see the pole for the American flag zip-tied to drape over my large pack. Above the large pack, I could see my waterproof bag riding atop the sissy bar. And these pieces were secured to the Lazy Rider bag, which I could feel against my back, between the sissy bar and me. You may not be able to pack in a way that allows you to see every item, but scan everything you can see while en route and double-check to be sure everything is still secure at each fuel stop.

Thoughts from the Road: Do the Important Things Now

My first day, the weather was gorgeous. Traffic flowed smoothly. During moments like that, I don't ask myself why I ride. Every minute, each sensation, reminds me how good it is to be outdoors; how great it feels to lean into a curve; how exhilarating even a momentary burst of acceleration can be.

Mirror check. Peripheral scan. Eyes front again. Everything looks good.

But even during moments like these—or maybe because of them?—I remember receiving a real wake-up call last year while re-reading *Your Money or Your Life*, by Joe Dominguez and Vicki Robin. The authors describe a financial strategy for early retirement.[14] Their goal is not retirement to be idle, but retirement to do things that bring satisfaction. Time to be with family. To build a boat. To see a part of the world you've never visited. To ride your motorcycle cross-country.

Mirror check. Peripheral scan. Eyes front. All's well.

Yet, so often our lives are completely out of balance. The things that matter *most* to us get the *least* time. The things that matter *least*, in the long run, get the *most* time. Our efforts to make a living overwhelm life itself. "Make a dying," Dominguez and Robin call this kind of employment. In the book, they point out:

> *As we moved from agriculture to industrialization, work hours increased, creating standards that label a person lazy if he or she doesn't work a forty-hour week.*[15]

Need to pass. Mirror check. Head check, look left. Confirmed clear. Go!

In the technology-heavy San Francisco Bay area, we're sometimes thought to be lazy if we don't work 70- or even 80-hour weeks. Pull all-nighters; crash under your keyboard on a foam pad; live on junk food and Jolt Cola until the project is done; until the quarterly projections are satisfied. What makes us so completely insane about work, whether in technology or a thousand other jobs? All I can imagine is that our identity—who we think we are—is too often tied to what we do; what we accomplish. As Rocky said to Adrienne in Stallone's first *Rocky* film, "I gotta prove I ain't no bum."

So, what's wrong with us? Maybe nothing, if our work is satisfying and the product is worthwhile. But that wake-up call

---

[14] Joe Dominguez and Vicki Robin, *Your Money or Your Life* (New York: Penguin Books, 1992).
[15] Dominguez and Robin, p. 222.

I mentioned earlier? It's this: Joe Dominguez died of lymphoma in January 1997—only five years after writing *Your Money or Your Life*.

Joe made time to do the things he cared about, including telling others to examine their lives—to be sure they were spending time on the things that matter most to them. Joe retired early. By living more simply, he "bought" time he otherwise would have spent working. That enabled him to do the things that mattered to him. Am I doing that, too? Are you?

Right now, I am. I'm on the way to see my children on the East Coast. I'm enjoying God's good earth spread out before Eli's handlebars. I'm breathing clean air, thankful for the warm sunshine.

Thank you, Joe, my friend. You are missed.

Chapter 3:

California Dreaming

Friday, December 7
Buttonwillow, CA to Blythe, CA—372 Miles

TRIP

The Trip:
Sand Storm!

California is just plain big. It's the third largest state in the Union, after Alaska and Texas. Los Angeles is the second largest city in the nation and a challenge in itself (my route crosses its outskirts). And the state is bordered to the east by mountains. Pick any pass you like, but you still must climb to get out of the state before you reach the relatively flat lands of Nevada or Arizona.

Given December weather, I couldn't risk crossing the U.S. mid-continent—the shorter, more direct route. To go south meant spending at least a day (or, as it turns out, two) just to get out of California and onto I-10, which crosses the bottom of the United States. Taking two days of this trip to leave California is quite different from breezing eastbound on I-80 to Reno in August. In only four hours on that trip, I had left the Redwood Empire,[1] ridden

---

[1] These days, Sonoma County is better known as Wine Country. However, its historic designation is the Redwood Empire from the large stands of redwoods that attracted settlers and lumberjacks to California's beautiful and rugged coast north of San Francisco Bay.

through Napa and the Central Valley, passed Lake Tahoe, and was through the Sierra before crossing into Nevada. By contrast, yesterday I spent all day just getting from Northern California to Bakersfield.

Made one business call this morning before leaving the hotel. My concession to Joe Dominguez' "making a dying." I'm tired this morning, too—not from riding, but as a result of not sleeping well. The room last night had a sticky, sweet smell like cheap air freshener. I downed my cottage cheese and checked out quickly following the call.

By the time I reached the intersection of California 58 and U.S. 395, I was ready for gas and a real breakfast. The Roadhouse Restaurant and Bakery, at "Four Corners"—Kramer Junction, CA— was a welcome site. And it didn't disappoint. Best Spanish omelet I've ever had, including mounds of guacamole and sour cream. Crisp bacon. Good coffee. Hash brown potatoes. Wheat toast, with an ample supply of Knott's Berry Farm jellies. Little did I know then it was a good thing I lingered to savor my breakfast. This meal would ultimately prove to be the highlight of the day.

After filling Eli's tank, I began the long downhill slope into metropolitan Los Angeles. I had already come through the Tehachapi Pass (snow on the tops of the hills, but not the road). Now, once through the Cajon Pass, the route begins a long, slow descent to San Bernardino. U.S. 395 to I-15, followed by I-215 and California Highway 30 would take me to I-10, my route for most of the trip across the U.S. The good breakfast and the prospect of getting into Arizona today lifted my spirits. Highway 30 offered some gorgeous sections, particularly just before University of the Redlands. Big Bear Lake is above this section of the highway and the peaks in that area were snow capped, easily visible from the road.

The wind picked up soon after leaving San Bernardino.

"Not a good sign," I thought.

Today's route goes through the San Gorgonio Pass near Banning. I've flown the Pass. It can be rough. The last time I was through here Susan and I were flying to an Aircraft Owners and Pilots Association (AOPA) meeting in Palm Springs. Part of our flight followed the same route I'm riding today. The wind through the pass creates uncomfortable turbulence for airplanes. Today, it was doing the same thing for motorcycles. I rode most of the way to Palm Springs leaned into the wind and trying to shelter myself behind the string of semis ahead of me. Werner Bausenhart did the same thing as he rode through Patagonia on his way to Tierra del Fuego.[2] I never thought I'd welcome riding behind tractor-trailer trucks, but today the truck-generated wind buffeting was calm compared to the gusts while riding in the open.

Stopped briefly for fuel. Making it to Phoenix still looks possible before dark. There's a short stretch from here to Indio, then 96 miles to Blythe and the state line. Next stop beyond Blythe, Phoenix!

Past Indio the wind grew even stronger. Having hung around a lot of airports and watched a few windsocks (which stand straight out at 15 knots), my guess is today's wind is 25–30 knots. It's coming from my left, with gusts significantly stronger than its constant 25–30 knots. I'm leaning about 10 to 15 degrees into the wind, just to maintain course. When the gusts catch the side of my full-face helmet, they involuntarily turn my head.

Then I saw it. It looked like a layer of fog, or maybe smog, in the distance. Whatever it was, it sat between me and the hills that mark the border of Southern California, along the Colorado River. As I rode closer, the air had an unfamiliar quality about it. I couldn't pin it down.

---

[2] Bausenhart, *Around the Americas*.

The wind grew stronger. Suddenly, conditions deteriorated rapidly. Sand storm! That's what it was. I'm enveloped! Sand is blowing across the road like drifting snow. It fills my helmet through the gap between my lips and the face shield. Visibility is down to two or three car lengths. And there is nowhere to go. I'm not going to stop and sit in the storm. Yet what will be the price of getting beyond it? A family member who lived in the desert once told me he had seen cars sanded to bare metal. Wind is driving the sand from my left, between Eli's two cylinders, and directly into the back of the air filter cover. Forget the paint—what about the engine? Will the air filter do its job? The windscreen is opaque, coated by a fine dust that accompanies the grit. How long will a bike run in these conditions?

It has been 20 minutes, the longest 20 minutes of the ride. The wind hasn't abated, but the air is starting to clear. I see hills near Blythe once again. Short of the hills I see a Union 76 truck stop. Eli and I stop for gasoline and to assess our condition. His sidestand groans as I extend it. Sand in the mechanism. The engine was running a bit rough when we stopped, but steadily. Will it start again? This encounter with the storm certainly means an unplanned stop in Phoenix or Tucson for an oil change. Everything is coated with a fine powder that seems to stick by electrostatic charge. I hope the dirt is the worst of it. No paint seems to have been sandblasted beyond polishing or repair.

In the midst of this, while standing in wind that snaps the flags to attention, the truck stop's pumps provide some comic relief. "C'mon!" I thought. "What else can happen?"

At Kramer Junction, the gas pump had refused to shut off—spewing gasoline over Eli and a good bit of the station before I could reach the shutoff lever. In contrast, these pumps are rigged to stop the flow and charge your credit card as soon as gas in the tank triggers the pump's auto-shutoff. That might work for cars and trucks, but Eli's 5.2-gallon tank has no filler neck and requires delicate topping off to fill completely. The pump's built-in intelligence has reduced tank capacity by probably 20 percent. I don't have the patience to insert my credit card and start over just to coax another two- or three-tenths of a gallon into the tanks. Blythe may be the end of the day, after all.

Stopping for gas after the sand storm

The bike restarts. I'm thankful. Eli and I press on, continuing to fight the wind—but no sand. My eyes and nose are full of grit. As I shut down the engine in front of Hampton Inn in Blythe, I realize the bike and I look about as ratty as we can. A quick once-over on my face with a bandana doesn't help much. What I need is a shower. Will they rent to someone who looks as bad as this? Smile and be cheerful. See how it goes. They rented.

After cleaning up, as well as getting some relief for my throat and lungs in the shower's mist, dinner became the next goal. Two restaurants were within walking distance. Sizzler's menu lists only iced tea or soft drinks. Sorry—not tonight! A big, cold beer is a must. The other restaurant, attached to the back of a coffee shop next to the motel, looks unlikely—but the hotel receptionist said it has a lounge. Let's try. I'm parched.

The Naugahyde-padded doors brought back memories of supper clubs I'd worked in as a musician in years gone by. Seating myself, a curious conversation began that completed today's long downhill ride.

"Beer?"

"Sure. We have everything." I breath a silent thanks.

"Sierra Nevada Pale Ale?"

"No, not everything like *that*. I meant we have Bud on tap and Heineken in bottles."

"Oh. Umm . . . then how about just a big glass of water? I'll order food in a minute, thanks."

In *The Hero with a Thousand Faces*, Joseph Campbell writes:

> *A hero ventures forth from the world of common day into a region of supernatural wonder; fabulous forces are there encountered and a decisive victory is won. The hero comes back from this mysterious adventure with the power to bestow boons on his fellow man.*[3]

No heroes here today. Just a tired, thirsty rider. I'll be glad to get out of California.

Dragging myself back to the motel, I noticed the wind had stopped and the sky was clear. I had hoped the ride would simplify

---

[3] Joseph Campbell, *The Hero with a Thousand Faces* (2nd ed.; Princeton: Princeton University Press, 1968), p. 30.

my life. Today was about as simple as it gets: stay upright and keep going. Maybe that says something about life, too. Still, as I fell into bed, some part of me looked forward to tomorrow. Faith. Hope. Love. Maybe that's how we keep going. The adventure continues.

Pre-Trip Preparation: The Art of Helmet Use

PREP

Think hard about helmets before you leave home. I know some states have no helmet law. My early days of motorcycling took place before any state made helmets mandatory. Riding parts of the southeastern U.S., as well as Hawaii, with no lid—it was great. But riding long distances at 75 mph for eight to ten hours a day, you may find comfort and safety more important than the local law.

On both trips, I took two helmets: a half helmet and a full-face helmet. Riders see and hear better when not impeded by a full-face helmet. No argument. I wear my half helmet when speeds and weather permit. With my shorty on, my peripheral vision is better, my hearing is sharper, and my attitude improves, too. But crossing a continent is different from a local jaunt or even a 200-mile cruise on a warm, sunny day. I was glad for my full helmet in the sand storm between Indio and Blythe!

I'm going to argue that—for the road—you will want a high-quality, full-face helmet. Why? First, because you *will* be safer. You don't want to end up on your chin at freeway speeds. A motorcycling friend who now lives in Colorado once told me, "Having your jaw wired shut for months while it heals, just doesn't sound like my idea of fun."[4]

Beyond safety, your ride will be more pleasant and less tiring. No half helmet, no earplugs, can match the quiet you'll enjoy in a

---

[4] E. C. Bell, Longmont, CO, friend and pastor.

full-face helmet with plugs. The difference is wind noise. A full-face streamlines the wind's passage around your head. Yes, some riders love hearing their pipes. But at 75 mph you aren't going to hear much from your pipes—Harley, Ducati, or otherwise—unless they are routed directly upward toward your ears. What you *will* hear is the endlessly tiring sound of hurricane-force winds rushing past your ears for eight or ten hours every day. And in a full-face helmet you'll also be better protected from rain, sand, flying objects, and even blinding sunlight at the beginning and end of each day.

Do full-face helmets have a downside? Absolutely. Even the best ones are heavy. And often the most comfortable are also expensive. You can't sneeze, scratch, blow your nose, or take a piece gum out of your mouth easily. And finally, a full-face helmet dictates a suiting-up sequence. Anything you want under the helmet (earplugs or a head rag) must go on first. You also need to complete buttoning or zipping up your jacket before donning your helmet, since you can no longer see your waist or chest because of the helmet's chin guard. Anything you can't do without sight becomes hopelessly clumsy. The first few times you forget and have to remove your helmet to complete the needed tasks—particularly in front of a crowd—you'll feel a bit foolish.

So, let's assume you're willing to take along a full-face helmet for its benefits. Is there anything you need beyond the helmet itself? The answer is, "Yes." If you ride a cruiser, you'll find that full-face helmets are designed for racers. Because racers lie on the bike's tank and look almost directly upward, face shields are set high in the helmet to provide visibility. To a cruiser, however, this space becomes a major annoyance. In my sofa-like slouch on Eli's seat, leaned back against my Lazy Rider bag, the top two or three inches of the helmet's face shield serve no purpose but to admit far too much early morning and late afternoon sun.

Thankfully, the solution is easy. Simply apply wide plastic tape over the unneeded section of the face shield. Cover about two inches, based on your preferences. But test your handiwork at road speeds. I tried white medical adhesive tape first, thinking it might reflect heat rather than absorb it. I also assumed it would be easier to remove (isn't medical tape designed to be pulled off skin without pain?). Bad idea. At 70 mph, the tape gradually crept up my face shield until it nearly blew off in a white wad. You'll find cheap plastic tape the color of the helmet, or black electrical tape, works best (see the figure, below). And, at least one commercial motorcycling product is also made for this purpose. See the ads in *Cycle World*, *Rider*, or any of the good motorcycle magazines.

Full-face helmet with tape strips on the visor

By the way, you may also want to cut a few short strips of tape and keep them handy for sunset and sunrise. At the beginning and end of each day, the sun's angle can be blinding for any rider. But with a little practice, you'll find that temporarily mounting one or two more short strips on the face shield has the same effect as a sun visor in your car. If the sun was to my side, I applied the tape strips vertically on the far right or left side of the shield. When riding directly into the sun, I would just add a piece to extend the downward reach of the band of tape at the top of my face shield.

And here are two final suggestions for perfecting your art of helmet use:

Get a Fog City Shield for inside your helmet.

This transparent layer of polymer adheres to the inside of the helmet's face shield and prevents it from fogging, or steaming up, during cold or wet weather.[5] The polymer causes a slight loss of clarity to night vision, but nothing compared to a cough or deep breath completely obscuring your view of traffic.

Keep a bandana or turtleneck handy.

Even in warm weather you'll appreciate this neck protection. Add a Schampa[6] neck gaiter if it's going to be cold. On Eli, the oncoming air flows almost vertically over the bike at exactly the spot where the bottom of my helmet opens to the wind. If your bike is similar, without something over your nose or around your neck when it's cold, you'll find out what ram-air injection can do to sensitive nostrils. You needn't ride with your nose covered constantly. But there will be times you'll appreciate having something to warm or deflect the air flow.

EQUIP

Your Equipment: Theft Protection

Theft protection is one of the most hotly debated topics in the motorcycling press. As recently as January and

---

[5] See *www.modernworld.com,* or get one from a local motorcycle dealer.

[6] Visit their online store at *www.schampa.com.*

February 2002, *American Motorcyclist* addressed motorcycle theft.[7] None of us wants to be among the small number of riders whose bikes are stolen while making a long journey.

What's the solution? The solution boils down to five items you can mix and match:

- Chains, locks, and cables
- Pre-installed devices like fork locks and keyed ignitions
- Your parking strategy
- Covers
- Alarms

Only *you* can determine *your* level of tolerance for risk. Clearly, the most conservative approach (in addition to other measures) is to lock your bike to an immoveable object, using a very heavy cable or chain. Without doing this, three or four determined thieves can steal any bike by simply lifting it into a truck.

The question is whether or not you want to devote valuable luggage space to that kind of gear. The answer for me was, "No." But part of that was philosophical. If we must constantly go to extraordinary lengths to protect ourselves against each other, the journey is no longer worth the effort. Prudence is one thing. Shackling my motorcycle to lampposts and motel stairways is another. And all of this ignores the fact that thieves seem remarkably ingenious at cutting chains, cables—even U-locks engineered specifically to defeat their efforts.

Instead, I adopted a careful parking strategy, and used all Eli's antitheft devices, including a bike cover and aftermarket alarm. After all, protecting our motorcycles is not terribly different from

---

[7] The publication of the American Motorcyclist Association, see *www.ama-cycle.org*.

protecting our homes and cars. A skilled thief, given sufficient time, can defeat even the most sophisticated theft protection. The key to prevention, then, is to deny thieves time and make their activities as conspicuous as possible.

Start by parking your bike in a well-lit, well-protected spot. Some motel clerks will allow you to park directly outside a window that faces Reception. If that's not possible, park directly outside your room—or if that is not possible, near an entrance or exit. But don't stop there.

A cover is a strong deterrent to thieves. A cover makes your bike far less visible, especially if you are riding a well-chromed Harley or a particularly attractive sport bike. On the other hand, thieves can't be certain what's under the cover. The bike may not be worth their attention. More important, just to find out, the thief is forced to devote extra time to uncovering your ride. Determining how to steal the bike—even if its worth stealing—is no longer a quick project.

Finally, by adding an alarm, you can further discourage investigation. Various shock-sensitive alarms are available. Check with your dealer or the ads in motorcycle magazines. Some alarms even come with pagers; if your bike is bumped, the alarm sounds and you are paged. In my experience, however, the paging feature is of limited value. If the alarm is set to be sensitive enough to recognize a fairly light touch—for example, someone lifting the edge of the cover—then even the contraction of engine parts cooling down after a ride or a strong gust of wind can set off the alarm. With the alarm set to its *least* sensitive state, I've never received a page. One could argue that's because the bike has never been knocked over or stolen. But 90% of the value of any alarm is the loud, audible alert that draws attention to the thief. Get a paging alarm, if you like, but count on the basics: park well, use your ignition and fork locks, cover your bike, and buy the loudest alarm you can find.

Riding Techniques:
Avoid Fixation

RIDE

Chapter 2 noted that riding a motorcycle is a little like making an instrument flight in an airplane. Your eyes must be constantly moving. If you have a disciplined scan—front, mirrors, and peripheral vision—you have taken a positive step toward heading off danger.

Pilots get into trouble if they stop their scan to fixate on one instrument. Fixation is just as dangerous for the motorcyclist. We must maintain our scan, even in the face of distractions. For example, when riding, I almost always wave to long-haul truckers I pass. Some are riders and, in any event, truckers do a difficult job well. I also hope that if they later see me broken down by the side of the road, they might remember the wave and stop to lend a hand. But part way into my second day on the road I realized my eyes were beginning to linger on my right-hand mirror as I passed each truck. I was fixating—not continuing my scan. Why? I wanted to see if the drivers returned my greeting, as many did, by flashing their lights.

The effect of pausing my scan could have been deadly. It takes less than a second for conditions to change ahead of your bike. I call this loss of concentration the "nanolapse." You know you've suffered a nanolapse when, at the instant your concentration returns, you realize that for just a fraction of a second, you weren't paying attention to handling the bike or managing the threats around you. Clement Salvadori addressed a similar phenomenon in his article titled "Mental Lollygagging."[8]

---

[8] Clement Salvadori, "Mental Lollygagging," *Rider* (February 2002), pp. 20-21.

What happens if a car brakes? An animal suddenly runs across the roadway? With my eyes stuck on my right mirror for even as little as a half second, the entire trip—perhaps even my life—might have ended.

Scan, scan, scan—front, mirrors, and peripheral vision. Don't let anything keep you from maintaining total situational awareness. If you suddenly hear a luggage strap flapping, don't try to fix the problem at 70 mph. Check your mirrors, signal, and get off the road. Do the same with any other distraction. You cannot afford to concentrate on only *one* thing while riding. Remember Keith Code's warning: you have only $10 worth of attention to spend.[9] If you spend it all on one distraction, one scenic vista, or even one daydream, your bike is effectively riderless. You're no longer an active part of setting its course and determining its safety—nor your own.

 ## Staying Organized: Take Your Time

One of the best organizing techniques on the road is simply to take a deep breath and say to yourself, "Take your time!" Packing a motorcycle is not a Zen thing, but when traveling by bike you quickly realize that most of us have become accustomed to the pace of a rush-order world. We expect everything to happen quickly. We slide into our cars, turn the key, and we're off. We may not even buckle our seat belt until we've backed out of the driveway and pointed the car toward our destination. We drive fast, talk fast, eat fast, and still complain about how much we failed to accomplish that day.

Life isn't meant to be lived like that and life on a motorcycle certainly is not. As a result, one of the most wonderful gifts your

---

[9] See "Riding Techniques" in Chapter 2.

ride will give you is the reminder that *it's OK to take your time*. You need to repack and mount luggage every morning. You have to don riding gear. You must do a pre-departure walkaround—checking tire pressures, double-checking the security of your luggage, and looking for any obvious problems (a fluid leak, a dangling bungee cord, a foreign object stuck in a tire). It's even OK to stare at your bike, appreciating how good it looks and how well designed it is to do the job you've asked it to do.

Even after you mount your bike, pause and look around. Did you drop anything as you boarded? Is there one last item you intended to stuff into a pocket, but you became distracted and forgot? Go slowly before departure to go fast later.

In the 21st century, *pace* frequently makes us insensitive to *place*. Let your trip be a reminder to slow down, look around, and breathe deeply. These aren't just rules for the road. You'll be amazed at how much better life looks when you don't slide behind the wheel and turn the key, intent only on the next destination.

Thoughts from the Road: Riding and Risks

When you decide to pursue a long distance ride, you will quickly hear from two distinct groups: folks who think it's the best idea they've heard in months, and others who tell you every story they can about the dangers of what you're about to do.

And let's face it. On a day like today, finding myself in the midst of unexpected conditions, my thoughts—as a prudent rider—turned to safety. You've likely had the same experience. What are the big risks and how can we avoid them?

For instance, you may have heard someone quote recent statistics that suggest the majority of motorcycle fatalities occur to older riders. Strictly speaking, that's untrue. I thought about this while riding and checked when I returned. Over a 10-year period,

1990–1999, the latest years for which the NHTSA has figures, the 20–29 year age group has consistently ranked number one in fatal accidents. What is true, however, is the number of fatal accidents involving older riders is increasing. The 30–39 and 40–49 age groups had 75–80% as many accidents as younger riders. In 1999, even the 49+ group had 52% as many accidents as the 20-year olds. Contrast this with only 13% as many accidents in 1990.

A partial explanation for the increased number of accidents among older riders is simply that more older riders own bikes today than they did 10 or 20 years ago. In 1980, riders over 30 owned only 36.9% of registered motorcycles. By 1990, that figure had increased to 59%. By 1998, riders over 30 owned a whopping 74.4% of all bikes.

Still, ownership statistics aside, it's worth remembering that as we age, our overall capabilities may decline compared to what we had it our twenties—strength, endurance, reaction time, vision, and hearing. So, after a day that would challenge even the safest rider, I was reminded that, for all of us who are over 30, we need to keep ourselves fit, work on our riding skills, and use the increased experience and judgment we have acquired to keep ourselves out of dangerous situations. And that might not be bad advice whatever our age—whether on or off our bikes.[10]

---

[10] See Appendix D for a complete discussion of accident statistics and what you can do to avoid becoming one.

Chapter 4:

Hotel California

Saturday, December 8
Blythe, CA to Tucson, AZ—279 Miles

TRIP

The Trip:
Road Sister

Two days to get out of California! As difficult as the late start Thursday and the sand storm yesterday had made the first couple of days, I'm leaving California today.

The coffee shop attached to last night's restaurant was well suited for breakfast. I bought a newspaper on the way in, hoping for a pleasant half-hour before hitting the road. But my hopes were shattered by a verbal standoff between the waitress and two motorists from L.A. What a thankless job waiting tables can be. I tipped well, hoping to let her know the rest of us appreciated her work. Maybe there ought to be a manners test before people are allowed to travel outside their own cities.

Happy to be back on Eli and in the fresh air, I quickly crossed the state line into Arizona. Almost immediately, rock formations along the highway began to jut skyward from the desert's surface. Arizona brought visual relief that the California desert had not. The road surface improved, too. Sadly, California—once the envy of the nation for its good roads, great weather, and free tuition for in-state college students—is rapidly becoming part of the third world. How do you resolve an impasse between citizens determined to limit taxes (maybe beyond the bounds of good sense) and a state government determined to overspend all limits? Another breakfast standoff. Just ride, I guess.

Today's first target was Chandler, AZ, south of Phoenix, where I had planned to stop for an oil change and checkup for Eli. But remembering the traffic Susan and I had encountered on a brief visit to Phoenix the previous March, when a sign suggested Highway 85 as a bypass to I-8 and Tucson, I happily diverted south. I-8 rejoins I-10 west of Tucson, thus making the bypass a shortcut, too. Steady wind, but no sand today. And this route certainly would be more pleasant than mid-morning traffic through the Phoenix metropolis.

Stopping on the shoulder where Highway 85 meets I-8, I turned on Eli's flashers and started to make a quick call home. Almost immediately, another bike joined me—a Harley Sportster, with a set of well-used leather saddlebags.

"Hey, you OK?" was the greeting. The ethic of stopping to assist stranded riders still exists among a good part of the motorcycling community.

"Yeah, fine. Just stopped to make a call."

"I ran out of gas a ways back. A couple in a Lincoln took me to the nearest station. The Sporty only holds three gallons. Against the wind I ran dry at 87 miles. You want to ride together for awhile?"

The Sportster's rider turned out to be on her way back to New Mexico, after going to the California coast to seek work on an oil-drilling rig.

"Not ready for women on their rigs yet," she said.

If so, it wasn't because she lacked guts! Even beyond its smaller tank, her Sportster had no windscreen and less weight to fight the gusts than Eli. Following her along I-8 toward Tucson, I admired her work keeping the bike into the wind and up to good road speeds. In her half helmet, aviator's goggles, and hair in a braid, she'd streamlined all she could for her push into today's headwinds. Sitting on Eli's 700 pounds, carrying almost twice as much fuel, and warm in a heated jacket liner and gloves, I was humbled. If my last two days were tough, I could only imagine what hers had been like.

A gallant man might have offered to trade rides for the next leg. I was so awestruck it didn't even occur to me. And in all likelihood, her response would have been, "Aw, this isn't bad. You should have been with me when...."

Ride safe, road sister.

Tucson Harley-Davidson was waiting when Eli and I arrived, thanks to having used the Harley Owners Group road atlas to find their number. They took Eli straight into the shop for service. In addition to changing his oil and filter, they found a slight gas leak from one of the fuel tank fittings. I was grateful for their quick, attentive care.

The quick turnaround also allowed me to reach Tucson Motorsports before the end of the day, a sister dealership on the outskirts of town. Tucson Motorsports specializes in sport bikes. Somewhere en route, the screw that secures the base plate that holds my helmet's face shield fell out. Depending on the make and construction of your helmet (I own a Shoei), take spare parts in your tool kit. The base plate itself failed later, in South Carolina. Shoei's quick release mechanism is convenient, allowing the rider to remove the face shield rapidly and without tools. But few, if any, Harley dealerships have such parts and a search in Greenville (my South Carolina destination) revealed that not every sport bike dealer stocks them, either.

With Eli and my helmet both happy, I stopped for the night in Tucson. Another day finished and—finally—out of California.

PREP

Pre-Trip Preparation: Rain Clothing

Think hard about rain before you depart. In my three trips across the U.S., two eastbound and one returning west, *none* was ever a completely dry trip. Without rain gear, your choices are either to be uncomfortable (and worry about your clothes drying overnight) or to sit out rainy days along the way somewhere in a place you may not want to be.

The first decision you need to make about rain suits is whether you prefer a one-piece suit, or a separate top and bottom. Generally speaking, my two-piece suit works well and is more comfortable and easier to put on than a one-piece outfit. The pants have a bib, which provides added protection from any rain that might sneak underneath the jacket.

You should try both types before deciding—unless you are planning to use a heated jacket liner. In that case, a two-piece rain suit becomes essential because the liner's electrical cord needs to exit your clothing somewhere near tank-level to connect to the electrical source. On my Harley, that connection was a pigtail wired to the battery, so the cord from the jacket liner had to connect to the pigtail at waist level. Cutting a hole through a one-piece suit was not an option.

Your second decision is whether you need a waterproof suit or one that is merely water resistant. For example, if you aren't comfortable riding in the rain and only plan to wear your suit long enough to get to the next restaurant or hotel, you don't need to invest as much as the rider who wants to keep riding and needs a completely waterproof suit. Materials range from proprietary fabrics like Gore-Tex and Cordura, to nylon, oilcloth, and rubberized materials. Again, your choice depends on whether you plan to ride long distances in your suit or simply escape the rain at the first possible opportunity. Oilcloth and rubberized materials are completely waterproof, but don't breathe and are not as comfortable as nylon or more expensive proprietary fabrics. On the other hand, oilcloth and rubberized materials are cheaper.

If you are considering one of the more expensive suits, concentrate more on the suit's maker than the material. I've used Gore-Tex jackets and pants that didn't block water at road speeds because they weren't made well (that isn't criticism of *all* Gore-Tex products, some of which work as expected). I've also had rain clothing made of no-name fabrics, manufactured by people who understood motorcycling, which kept me completely dry.

A tight-fitting jacket collar helps. Ignore jackets with built-in hoods. While the hood's utility when you are off your bike seems attractive, a hood generally makes the neck of the jacket too bulky to be comfortable with a full-face helmet. If you unpack the hood to reduce the bulk, it becomes a sail that will constantly annoy you by flapping against your helmet. The ultimate wet-weather neck protection hasn't been invented. I'd like a waterproof gaiter that joins the bottom of my helmet to my rain jacket. That would enclose my neck in the small "tent" formed by connecting the helmet to the gaiter. Run-off would be channeled down over my jacket—instead of down my neck. In all my travels and research, I haven't seen anything like this.

With your top and bottom covered, the third and final decision is whether to go with waterproof boots or boot gaiters. Waterproof boots are heavy for dry weather and walking around town. On the other hand, ordinary boots admit rain and can be soaked after riding in the wet. My solution was to buy a pair of Harley's boot gaiters. These slip on over ordinary boots. They have a rubberized sole up front, but the heel of the boot is left open for using the motorcycle foot pegs. The gaiters also have additional water protection on the shin and toe where the rain strikes hardest.

All in all, the gaiters proved perfectly satisfactory in all wet conditions, from light mists to hard rain.

Preparing to ride in the rain can be expensive. You can expect to pay $200 or more for a breathable waterproof jacket, and between $150–200 for waterproof pants with a bib that extends up under your jacket. Aerostich suits made from Gore-Tex and Cordura run even higher—as much as $700–800—but have the reputation of being the finest rain gear available.[1] At the other end of the spectrum, you can find inexpensive oilcloth or rubberized suits for less than $100. Boot gaiters run between $50–100. So, consider how much you plan to ride in the rain and how long you will keep the suit, before investing.

EQUIP

Your Equipment: Vibration

Let's spend a few minutes talking about "the shakes." All motorcycles vibrate. The only question is, "how much?" Read the road tests. You'll find descriptions that range from "a buzz," to "a tingling," to "almost vibration free" (the key word being "almost"). Harley-Davidsons have the reputation for vibrating the most. If your bike vibrates, can you launch cross-country with confidence?

Frankly, I've ridden BMW boxers that seemed to vibrate more than my Softail, but I don't want to start a culture war. Maybe the BMW was badly tuned. Harleys can vary, too. For example, my first ride on a counter-balanced Twin Cam B engine was disappointing. Susan and I rented a Heritage Softail in Chicago with the B-series engine and rode it to Milwaukee for a rally. The level of vibration

---

[1] Learn more about Aerostich products at their site, *www.aerostich.com*. And, for anyone tired of legalese, spend a few minutes reading the Fine Print section of their Copyright and Disclaimer page. You'll go away smiling.

was higher than my Evo-engined Softail. On the other hand, I recently tried a friend's Road King and found the rubber-mounted engine (a standard Twin Cam without balancers) was almost turbine-like, it was so smooth.

The point? Just this: some road tests seem to suggest a persistent buzz in the foot pegs or bars is a nearly fatal flaw. Thankfully, Eli has one of the smoothest non-balanced, rigid mounted engines I've ridden—but there is still enough vibration to blur the mirrors and tingle the rider's feet through the pegs. Fatiguing? Maybe. I can't say, having never crossed the country on a Gold Wing or BMW K1200 LT. However, I find that by changing the position of my boot on the peg, the vibration against my foot is redirected—creating the pleasant sensation of a massage, rather than feeling any annoying tingle. Ditto for my hands. Just change hand positions occasionally. Of course, some people have no special love for massage. Pick your ride accordingly.

One qualification needs to be made, of course. We are talking here about normal engine vibration. If your bike exhibits any fork shimmy or abnormal engine vibration, have your bike checked carefully before riding anywhere.

Riding Techniques: Relax!

RIDE

If you can't relax on your bike, it's going to be a long ride. What does "relax" mean? It means being comfortable, most of all. Regardless of your riding position—upright, laid back, or lying on the tank—you shouldn't feel any tension, while still remaining engaged and fully in control of the bike. If you dismount every night and need a hot tub for your shoulders, then you weren't relaxed. Here are some techniques you can use to get—and stay— relaxed while you ride.

Say the magic words

Muscle tension is not limited to motorcycle riders, of course. Runner Jeff Galloway devotes an entire chapter of his book to discussing "magic marathon words"—the first of which is "relax."[2] He argues that if we are uncomfortable, the self-protective, rational left side of our brain takes over and sends messages that make conditions seem worse than they really are. Whether that's the case or not, you *can* learn to relax. For example, by simply telling yourself to "relax" from time to time, you catch and release the unconscious tension that builds up.

Keep a light touch

One of the best ways to prevent muscle tension is to maintain a light touch on the bars. The most effective steering technique is almost always "push-push." Push left to go left; push right to go right. If you haven't studied counter-steering—why the bike goes left when you push on the left bar (which actually points the front wheel to the right)—you should. Consider enrolling in Keith Code's cornering school.[3] His "No BS Bike" ("*no body steering*") debunks the myth about weight transfer starting a motorcycle's lean into a corner.

But the point here is regardless of your understanding of counter-steering, a light "push to turn-push to return to straight" is far superior for control—as well as muscle relief—compared with a tense grip and rigid forearms that "jerk-jerk."

Notice in the photo at right, the rider pushed the *right* handlebar (right viewed from his perspective). Note, too, he is leaned to the right and the bike is turning right, around the cone. The front wheel, however, is pointed to the *left*. As counter-intuitive

---

[2] Jeff Galloway, Marathon: *You Can Do It* (Bolinas, CA: Shelter Publications, 2001), p. 85.
[3] See *www.superbikeschool.com*.

1. Push right

3. Turning right

2. Front wheel pointing left

Counter-steering demonstrated in dirt-bike training

as all of this may seem, it works. You initiate the turn by pushing right to go right. The photo exaggerates the angle of the front wheel, because the rider is also sliding to scrub off speed.

Vary hand position and use cruise control

Change your hand position on the bars, too. This is easier on some bikes than others. By providing multiple places that the rider can put his or her hands, different muscles are used and numb spots don't develop as easily. For long trips you should also install and use some sort of cruise control on your bike. Most Harleys provide a poor man's version of cruise control via a thumbscrew near the handgrip on the throttle side. Older bikes, of course, do not have government-mandated throttle return springs, so their throttles remain open until deliberately rolled closed.

If your bike doesn't have some version of cruise control, check with your dealer or with aftermarket vendors about installing such a system. On Eli, tightening the thumbscrew locks the throttle open, without making it impossible to roll off power in an emergency. As a result, on relatively empty stretches, I could set whatever speed was comfortable and then wrap my thumbs around the mirror stems, relaxing my fingers and extending them forward. You'll find your own favorite hand positions. Even installing something as simple as the Throttle Rocker[4] offers a way to change your hand position and lessen the tension in your wrist and forearm from constant throttle application.

Change body position

Finally, don't forget to change positions occasionally on the seat to redistribute your body weight. One reason I recommend Don Hood's Lazy Rider bag is because the bag makes changing positions on the seat so easy. I could brace my feet against the forward control pegs, put my shoulder blades against the Lazy Rider bag, and actually lift my backside entirely off the seat. When I settled in again, even if it was into almost the same position, the tender parts always felt a good bit better! If you're riding a cruiser-style bike with a sissy bar against which the Lazy Rider can rest, give the Lazy Rider a try.

Thoughts from the Road: Cutting Free

"A major departure like this is never easy," Ben Carlin wrote.[5]

Of course, he was writing of a significantly more complex and dangerous journey. Australian Carlin and his wife Elinore crossed the Atlantic Ocean in a military surplus Jeep. Yes, an amphibious

---

[4] See *www.throttlerocker.com*, for Throttle Rocker Motorcycle Accessories, Scotts Valley, CA. At $10, their device is a great bargain for any bike without cruise control or a thumbscrew to hold the throttle in a constant position.

[5] Ben Carlin, *Half Safe: Across the Atlantic by Jeep* (London: André Deutsch Limited, 1955), p. 47. The book has long been out of print, but you can usually locate a used copy through *www.abebooks.com*, one of the most useful sites on the Web—for book lovers, at least.

Jeep. Yes, across the Atlantic. And, as preposterous as the story sounds, it is absolutely true. His book is fascinating, as are the difficult-to-find sequels—one by Carlin and one by Boyé Lafayette De Mente.[6]

But Ben didn't stop with simply crossing the Atlantic. With a bit of coaxing and cleaning up after arrival, he *drove* the Jeep out of the water and partway across northern Africa and Europe! Continuing from Paris, he took the Jeep to Istanbul, Tehran, Delhi, and Calcutta—reentering the water to reach Rangoon. From there, his stops included Bangkok, Saigon, the Philippines, Japan, the Aleutians, and Alaska, for a complete circumnavigation of the globe by sea and land.

Ben was right. A major departure like this *is* never easy. Clearing your schedule, explaining the trip to others, assembling the gear, preparing your bike, and checking your skills, all take time. But think of it as *creating* time. Once the bike is packed and you fire up the engine, you're on no one's schedule but your own. You answer to no one but yourself. You are free!

Ben also wrote, "There are a hundred and one details to be attended to in cutting yourself free from the ridiculous trappings and entanglements of civilized existence."[7]

I've carved out time for this trip. You'll have to do the same. Yet probably for both of us, the prospect of even being temporarily free from the trappings and entanglements of existence beckons. The allure is not a shirking of responsibility. Instead, a long trip by motorcycle offers the chance to step outside the shallowness and pretense that so creeps into our daily lives. On the road, there

---

[6] Ben Carlin, *The Other Half of Half-Safe* (Guilford, Western Australia: Guilford Grammar School Foundation, Inc., 1989) and Boyé Lafayette De Mente, *Once a Fool: From Japan to Alaska by Amphibious Jeep.* Insofar as I know, this book is available only as a download from *www.hadami.com/bookinfo/details.asp?bookID=114*.

[7] Carlin, *Half-Safe*, p. 47.

are no office politics. On the road, no one cares if your house is bigger or smaller than someone else's. On your bike, the color of your new car, your parachute, or your skin matters less than how well you ride.

Take a deep breath—and go ride.

Chapter 5:

Deep in the Heart of Texas
Sunday, December 9
Tucson, AZ to Ft. Stockton, TX—554 Miles

The Trip:
"Aren't you cold, honey?"

TRIP

Tucson is a nice town, but Arizona's urban areas have spread the way Los Angeles did years earlier. Surrounded by the Santa Catalina Mountains rising 9,000 feet to the north and the Rincon Mountains to the east, Tucson is visually stunning. But its size is daunting. If you include Davis-Monthan Air Force Base, home of the Desert Lightning Wing and the largest dry-storage facility for aircraft in the world, Tucson covers more than 500 square miles. After his oil change and a night in the city, Eli and I were ready for a place with a more human scale.

Sundays at home I'd be in church. You'd think in 500 square miles, I'd have found a church here. After reviewing the options, I picked one in Catalina, just outside Tucson. Catalina was in the wrong direction for making progress on the trip but passing by Catalina State Park on a sunny Sunday morning seemed like a pleasant prospect.

However, I had missed one important fact. On this particular Sunday, the Tucson Marathon was being run on the exact route to get to the church. At 9:00 a.m., as the church's service was going to start, I still hadn't reached Catalina. It was time to turn back and point the front tire toward El Paso. Texas, here we come.

The wind still hadn't let up. At times yesterday, the gusts twisted Eli's windscreen to the point I wondered if its quick-release mounts might fail. Wind from the 10 o'clock position to our left appeared to fold the top of the windscreen toward my right shoulder. How good are the mounts? Could the windshield come off and become a lethal projectile, like a tree limb in a tornado? That thought wasn't a pleasant one.

The route climbed from an altitude of 2,400 feet at Tucson to 4,200 feet at Lordsburg, NM. Exiting for gas, food was also on my mind. The Grapevine Café appeared to be a popular spot for the Sunday lunch crowd. The parking lot was nearly full, as was the restaurant. Stepping inside, I took one of the last open booths. It felt good to be off the bike. It was cold outside, despite my heated gloves and jacket liner, especially crossing the 4,935-foot summit at Texas Canyon. It was cold inside, too—with lots of curious stares, but few smiles. I was a leather-clad anomaly, out of place among these folks, men in their Western hats and women in flowered dresses. There was no way they could know we have more in common than appearance suggested: respect for independence, self-reliance, personal responsibility, and trust in God. I paid for the meal, used the Grapevine's clean restrooms to put on my outerwear, and headed for I-10 and Texas.

El Paso sits along the Rio Grande where, flowing south from New Mexico, the river turns east. Settled as early as 1598, this bend in the waters marks a stopover that has attracted gunfighters, goldrushers, and gamblers—as well as the city's current cosmopolitan population. The parts of the city that stretch along I-10 don't make for a particularly pleasant ride, but I hoped to have more time to sample El Paso's cross-cultural character on the return trip. Tanked up west of town and kept moving.

Beyond El Paso the towns are smaller and widely separated. The challenge now would be finding a place to stop, while being careful not to exceed the range of Eli's 5.2-gallon tank in the dark. This would be the first night I'd ridden any significant distance after dark.

As night fell, the sky was clear. The haze enveloping El Paso was left behind. "The stars at naht, are big and braht; deep in the heart of Tex-as." "They truly *are* big and bright," I thought. It was awe-inspiring to be under this glorious night sky. Eli was running smooth and fast. I was warm in my heated jacket and gloves. With the motorcycle humming contentedly, I pondered riding all night but thought better of it. Gas options would be much more limited late at night than during the day.

Miles passed contentedly. It had been a while since I'd seen any sign of a town—much less an open gas station. I was already beginning to be seriously concerned when, almost like a mirage, a dim sign for food and gas appeared in the distance. With a sigh of relief, I resolved not to push my luck again by riding in some of the most deserted stretches of the western U.S. without a plan. Riding this stretch prompted some interesting thoughts about how I might have to make camp beside a fuel-exhausted motorcycle. Would the engine's warmth protect me from the cold Texas night, and for how long? What sort of wildlife roams West Texas, and would it be curious about a sleeping figure beside the road? To what extent does the planet's most vicious predator—man—roam these roads at night, preying on those who have been foolish enough to run out of gas?

Thankfully, the station wasn't a mirage. The pumps were the old fashioned kind, marked "Pay Inside." I took advantage of this opportunity to use the café's restrooms and make a quick call home. Susan seemed a bit concerned at how late it was and my not being able to say exactly where the station was located. She was following my route using MapQuest and a road atlas, trying to estimate how far—and how long—to the next potential stopping spot. On this stop I'm afraid I gave her inaccurate information and she worried when my next call was much later than expected.

The café was already closed or I'd have eaten, too. While inside, I pulled small plastic trash bags over my socks and re-laced my boots. For the first time tonight, the wind chill had gotten to my feet. Maybe the layer of plastic will insulate a bit more than cotton socks and the boots themselves.

Sitting in a deserted part of the café and slipping on my boots, a woman ask the cashier, "Who's riding the motorcycle?" Blond and attractive, she and another woman were driving an enormous pickup, towing a good-sized horse trailer.

"Aren't you cold, honey?" she asked, as we passed outside by the pumps.

"Florida or Bust" was written in the accumulated road grime on one of the truck's windows. Clearly, they were headed for warmer territory.

"It's not bad," I answered. But it was. The woman smiled and pulled her door closed. I could see bags of snacks and drink cans on the back seat in the king cab. Now I was hungrier than before. Worse still, I was cold inside, too. I missed Susan and didn't relish another night alone. What next? Just ride.

The layer of plastic in my boots was not terribly effective at highway speeds. I resorted to warming my feet against Eli's exhaust collector on the right side and his primary case on the left. Traveling these dark, largely deserted stretches of Texas, I was grateful for Eli's warmth and absolute reliability. His big twin engine hummed on as we motored through the clear night.

In the distractions and chill of our last stop, I'd neglected to put in my earplugs. The wind noise and my cold feet became increasingly annoying. To stop, take off my helmet, and insert earplugs would only make me colder. I decided to stop at the next reasonable opportunity. We exited at Ft. Stockton without signaling. The roads were empty. After cruising the main street to review motel options, the Swiss Clock Inn looked best. Most promising of all was its restaurant, which looked as if it might still be open. Maybe there was still hope for food before turning in for the night.

No such luck. The restaurant was closed. My assigned room was on the windswept backside of the motel. As I dragged my bags up the metal stairway to the room, the night air cut through my jacket more deeply than it had on the road. And I was hungry. Stopped at a vending machine in the hallway. What do you suppose "aren't you cold, honey" had to eat in her big, warm truck? As I ate my peanuts and drank motel coffee brewed in the room, crossing America on a motorcycle didn't seem very exciting tonight.

But the stars had been beautiful. Morning would come. And I knew that when it did, Eli would fire up and idle contentedly. I would load my bags, let out the clutch, and everything would be all right again.

PREP

Pre-Trip Preparation:
Eye Protection, Hand Protection

Chapter 3 discussed helmet use. I hope you are convinced that riding long distances at high speeds warrants a full-face helmet.

But, if you also heed my suggestion to carry two helmets—a full-face and a half helmet—you will find many times to wear the shorty. Perhaps you've arrived at your destination and you're just cruising around town. Or maybe you have slowed down for the evening. As you idle through the soft, evening air and taking time to enjoy the sights, sounds, and smells, you don't want the coverage nor do you need the aerodynamic protection of a full-face helmet.

Protecting your eyes

With a short helmet on, however, pay extra attention to eye protection. Riding without glasses or goggles is an unnecessary invitation to injury. An almost unlimited selection of eyewear, prescription and nonprescription, is available.

The most important functions of motorcycling eyewear are to keep the wind from producing tears and to prevent foreign objects (bugs, stones, and other debris) from entering your eyes. I wear prescription lenses for distance, so I—like you, maybe—have fewer choices in eyewear than someone with 20/20 vision. Still, I've found ordinary plastic frames that sit directly on my nose block enough wind to keep my eyes from making tears. A variety of shapes and styles are available in plastic frames. Check with your local optician.

When you have found comfortable frames that block the wind, be sure the lenses are high-impact plastic. Although very few opticians supply glass lenses these days, make sure your plastic prescription lenses are well fitted in the frame. Advise whoever does your glasses that these are going to be used on a motorcycle. If your optical store uses an external lab to grind the lenses, have your optician check the fit for accuracy and tightness.

You may even want to consider special sports glasses, like squash or racquetball players use. These have lenses that are fitted in the frames in an especially secure way to guard against impact from an errant shot. Finally, custom motorcycle glasses and goggles are available from vendors that advertise in most motorcycle magazines. These tend to be more expensive than other options, but offer styles you may find appealing.

None of these solutions guarantees 100% satisfaction, but if you make careful, conscious choices about the type of eye protection and how it is produced, you'll have the best chance of warding off typical problems of wind, bugs, and debris.

During the daytime, of course, you'll almost certainly want sunglasses, regardless of your helmet preference. In addition to all the medical warnings about sunglasses protecting us from ultraviolet rays, they just make seeing easier. If you require corrective lenses, work with a good optician to find a pair that works with your half helmet, as well as under your full-face helmet. Your full-face helmet has less space for the temple pieces that must squeeze between the helmet's padding and your head. You'll want to be sure the temple fit is comfortable for all your glasses before starting on a long trip.

Sunglasses and half helmet do the trick

At night, of course, you still need eye protection. Riders who require prescription lenses should have a pair of glasses similar to their sunglasses for use after dark. But riders with 20/20 vision still need eye protection. If you are riding with a full-face helmet, your face shield does everything necessary—assuming it is down, not up to admit air. If you are wearing your half helmet, however, you should consider untinted glasses with plano (non-prescription) lenses. An optician can help you purchase such glasses. Once again, be sure the glasses sit directly on your nose and snugly against your face and forehead. This fit blocks the wind, as well as preventing tears and blurred vision.

One last note about glasses: consider having two sets of each kind you plan to use. Glasses are easy to lose or break and you don't want to get halfway across the country and need an optician. Keeping track of your glasses, especially if you don't need to wear them all the time, is an important step to add to your staying organized routine. See "Staying Organized" in Chapter 1 for some ideas.

Protecting your hands

Protecting your eyes seems obvious; the need to protect your hands may be less obvious. Yet, if your hands are hurting, every action from rolling on power to pumping gas to removing bungee cords will be painful. Hand creme is more important than you might imagine. Sounds odd, maybe, given the image of bikers. But be certain to take industrial-strength hand protection on your trip. By the time I reached Texas, my hands were chapped and bleeding at the knuckles—despite spending most of every day in gloves. Unless you have more dexterity in gloves than I do, you still need to remove your gloves to tie boots, locate change in your pocket, insert your credit card in pay-at-the-pump stations, and tighten and loosen straps when loading/unloading luggage. When you remove your gloves, the zippers on your jacket pockets (or something else) will claw at already dry, chapped skin. And all of this ignores any work you do on your bike while traveling, or the results of overfilling a tank and having gasoline drench your hands.

You may hate the greasy feeling, but rub on the creme and preserve your hide. Eucerin Moisturizing Creme—the heavy stuff, not the lighter lotion—works pretty well. Or you may have a favorite creme/cleaner that you use around your shop. Just pack whatever you take in a location where you can get to it frequently. You'll want it for a summer ride, too. While summer is marginally easier on the hands, riding without gloves, fuel spills on your hands, too much sun without sunscreen, or working on your bike cause the same problems.

Your Equipment: Avoiding Dehydration

EQUIP
You've heard the saying, "You are what you eat." That is never truer than when you are on the road. Skip a couple of meals or forget to drink enough water, and you'll quickly realize that food and water are just as much a part of your "equipment" as your jacket or gloves. And, I'd suggest that water is the more important of these two elements. Drink, drink, drink!

How much is enough?
Most people don't drink as much water as they should. The human body is 75% fluids, fluids that depend on getting enough water—not Coca-Cola, not coffee, and not beer or wine—into your system. As refreshing as other beverages may be, they are no substitute for water. In fact, alcohol and caffeine act as diuretics, causing you to lose the healthy fluids needed for maintaining a healthy body.

When you don't give your body the amount of water it needs, dehydration results. Ron Ayres, sixth place finisher in the 1995 round-the-U.S. Iron Butt Rally reports that the warning to stay adequately hydrated was among the more valuable pre-rally tips participants received.[1]

How much water is enough? Most nutritionists or doctors recommend about eight eight-ounce glasses of water daily. That's roughly two liters of water per day. Wilderness survival training emphasizes you need that much water even in cool areas and with relatively little physical activity.[2] Add heat, exertion, or stress, and the need goes up. Motorcyclists also must replace the extra amount demanded by the drying effects of the wind. Combine all this with the low humidity in the western U.S. (all over the U.S. in winter), and two liters a day is probably not enough.

Finding time to drink enough

This immediately raises the question, "How you gonna find time to ride, if you gotta drink that much?" There are a couple of answers. One is to do most of your hydration in the mornings and evenings. Yes, cup and water bottle holders can be rigged to traveling bikes. Some bikes even have built-ins. But that misses the point. What goes in must come out. The limit on what we can drink while riding is how often you can afford to stop and still put in decent mileage during the day.

I found I could drink one-third to one-half my daily amount of water before departure in the morning and be comfortable until my first gas stop—roughly 150 miles later. As the automobile disclaimers say, "Your mileage may vary." However, I also found that, continuing to re-hydrate at each gas stop rapidly increased the urgency associated with the need to stop. Distances dropped

---

[1] Ayres, *Against the Wind*, p. 40.
[2] See *www.wilderness-survival.net/chp6.php* for more information on this topic.

to as little as 75–80 miles between stops, with some of that mileage being uncomfortable.

By drinking, say, one-third of my daily needs before departure and then not drinking a significant amount again until evening, the distance between stops was steady at about 150 miles. (In no-wind conditions on the flats, Eli's tanks are good for more than 200 miles, but slightly more frequent breaks help me maintain better alertness and more consistent road speeds.) Then, upon arrival at my evening stop, I would be careful to drink an additional one-third or so of the targeted daily amount. Finally, before bed—even during the night occasionally, in exceptionally dry locations—I would finish the remainder of the day's allotment and then start the same procedure again the next morning.

One important note of caution, however: this technique only works on winter rides or in relatively temperate conditions. During hot weather rides, drink constantly! Horst Haak, an Iron Butt rider who avoided fluid until one hour before planned food and fuel stops, came dangerously close to suffering the effects of heat exhaustion and dehydration during his trip across the Southwestern U.S.[3] Dehydration is unpleasant and debilitating. Don't risk it.

And then when you've had enough...

There is an answer, however, that allows you to drink constantly: the E-Z Leaker.[4] The device is hard to discuss without a smile. How can you not love a company whose logo includes the abbreviation E-Z-P? Made for men and women, the Leaker uses a cup- or condom-like device appropriate to your gender. A tube straps to

---

[3] Ayres, *Against the Wind*, p. 96.

[4] See *www.ezleaker.com* or David Edwards' highly entertaining editorial in the August 2001 issue of *Cycle World*. As this book goes to press, by the way, E-Z Leaker has announced its plans to discontinue operations. Constructing a similar device from medical supplies and plastic tubing would not be difficult.

your leg using Velcro straps provided. You have an option whether you want the tube to terminate in a storage bag near your boot or simply to direct the stream down and away from the bike. Morris Kruemcke, on a Honda Gold Wing, employed a similar device in the 1995 Iron Butt Rally. "Morris claimed that the real advantage of the device was not that it eliminated frequent stops, but that it eliminated the tendency some riders have to dehydrate themselves by not drinking enough fluids."[5] Drink, drink, drink!

E-Z Leaker advertisement

---

[5] Ayres, *Against the Wind*, p. 33.

Having tried the E-Z Leaker, let me offer these observations. For some people the greatest barrier will be the sensation of just "letting fly" while fully clothed. That breaks every rule we have been taught from the time our parents housetrained us. Once you get past that, the device works wonderfully, but proved difficult to keep in place when not sitting (for example, while loading luggage, checking tire pressures, or walking into and out of mini-marts and service stations). Perhaps more practice would have cured my mounting problems.

In the end, however, I found that slightly more frequent fuel stops did not affect the day's mileage. If distances were 125–150 miles between fuel stops based on the morning-and-evening routine suggested earlier, versus 150–200 miles with the Leaker in place, I didn't gain enough time to make using the device worthwhile. Your conclusions could be very different if you are accustomed to stopping much more often, or if you are trying to stay with a group that stops infrequently.

The point is, whatever it takes, drink enough water to stay healthy throughout your trip. You may not find it difficult to compensate for only one or two days' water deficit. But after that, you begin to risk your health, and with it, the success and enjoyment of your trip.

RIDE

Riding Techniques: Dealing with Trucks

Let's talk about trucks. You won't need more than a day's travel to realize big rigs deserve special attention. The turbulence they generate at road speeds will get your attention fast. Anticipation, technique, and confidence in your bike are the keys to successfully sharing the road with your bigger brothers.

Anticipating turbulence and other dangers

You can learn to anticipate the severity of turbulence near big rigs create. Think about the times when, as a kid, you held your hand out the car window. If it was flat (palm parallel to the road surface) it made a nice wing-like device. Later model semis, with fairings on the tractor cab, direct air up over the trailer and increase gas mileage through streamlining. Conditions while riding behind and passing trucks like this is fairly predictable.

On the other hand, remember what it was like to put your hand outside the car when you made a fist or stuck out your fingers like a spider web. The more oddly shaped the truck is, the greater the odds its turbulence will be severe and unpredictable. Tank trucks, car carriers, and flatbed trailers loaded with odd objects deserve extra attention.

Anticipating truck turbulence helps you whether you are following, passing, or being passed by a truck. In general, avoid following trucks if at all possible. Trucks can be particularly dangerous (without intending to be) if a tire disintegrates. Remember seeing the fragments of rubber carcasses of truck tires along the highway? Imagine the impact if one strikes you at 70 mph. You're much more likely to be affected if you are behind rather than in front of the truck. Just get past.

Passing with confidence

After anticipation, technique for getting past trucks counts most. First, *never* linger when passing! Remember the Motorcycle Safety Foundation course that told you to maintain at least two seconds separation ("one-thousand one, one-thousand two") from vehicles in front of you? When something breaks into that two-second bubble of protective space—like having a truck immediately beside you as you pass—you need to move smartly to restore your protective space.

Anticipate turbulence and pass quickly

Next, use this two-step procedure for a greater feeling of control when passing a truck:

- First, accelerate to higher-than-passing-speed, as you move from behind the truck to the left-hand lane. If you were maintaining at least two seconds separation behind the truck, you have plenty of time to accelerate.

- Second, as your bike enters the turbulence near the left-rear corner of the semi trailer, momentarily roll off power to shift weight to the bike's front fork. The effect of this maneuver plants the fork and front tire more solidly—avoiding the feeling of insecurity that results if you continue to accelerate with a lighter front-end through buffeting winds.

If slowing down ever so briefly sounds counterintuitive, don't worry. With practice, the entire procedure becomes one seamless movement. Just roll on the power, then roll off for a fraction of a second when you hit the turbulence, and finally plow on through.

Staying Organized: Plan Ahead

At the risk of belaboring the obvious, part of staying organized is thinking about where you'll be next, and what you and your bike will need. At the most basic level, you'll need food and gas. Eating peanuts and drinking motel-room coffee happened because I didn't adequately organize the last four to five hours of my day. Similarly, if the café and filling station had not miraculously emerged out of the darkness, Eli would have exhausted his reserves and I wouldn't have had even peanuts and coffee.

No matter how carefully you prepare before leaving home, and no matter how many times you review your daily mileage targets with an eye toward the availability of services, you will face unanticipated decisions about food, gas, changing weather, traffic conditions, and lodging. In retrospect, and despite the glory of the stars seen from the West Texas desert, my foray into the night was ill advised.

I'm not suggesting you pre-select every fuel stop and hotel. In fact, quite the opposite should be the rule. The freedom to go at our pace and stop when we like is among motorcycling's many pleasures. But don't ride blindly, indifferent to your needs and the needs of your bike. Before continuing beyond your tentative overnight destination (as I did, going beyond El Paso), be sure you know where your next opportunity for lodging may be. I should have done this at my gas stop east of El Paso, but didn't. Also, think about what traffic you may encounter. I should have done so later in the trip, when my desire to keep riding put me in Atlanta's unpleasant rush hour traffic.

Plan far enough ahead to give you peace. Much of our reason for riding is to attain that peace—the mental and emotional space where we gain respite from daily cares. So protect it. It's easy to become intoxicated with the freedom and sense of movement that brings such peace. Just remember that peace comes partly from planning. Being stranded out of gas and food with no place to sleep from a lack of planning causes that peace to vanish quickly.

Thoughts from the Road: Riding as Overcoming

Why do we push beyond our limits? Why cross America on a motorcycle? Why do anything difficult, uncomfortable, inconvenient, or potentially dangerous?

No one would suggest that crossing a continent on a motorcycle is the ultimate test of courage. That would be an affront to our true heroes. Still, our journeys have the potential to open our eyes and to confront our anxieties.

In his study of courage, author William Miller says courage is "a proper overcoming of fear properly felt."[6] To fly blindly in the face of risk requires no courage, only a death wish. But what about overcoming? Do we exercise courage only when we save a child who has fallen into a river? Go to war? Rescue the injured in times of natural disaster? These acts do require overcoming fears and our heartiest thanks should go out to men and women who continually put themselves in harm's way for our sakes.

But could overcoming begin more simply? In our post-9/11 world, could the beginnings of overcoming simply mean abandoning the mindset that comfort, convenience, and security are basic rights? We fear airplanes, because they *may* crash. We won't ride

---

[6] William Ian Miller, *The Mystery of Courage* (Cambridge, MA: Harvard University Press, 2000), p. 19.

motorcycles, because a rider *could* be injured. We cling to jobs we hate, because quitting *might* result in financial insecurity.

We forego attainable dreams, because someone *could* look askance. We avert our eyes from opportunities for public service and ministry, at home and abroad, because such work *might* be difficult. We skip meat, swallow cholesterol-lowering drugs, make excuses for not exercising, and rush to therapy to plaster over our gaping canyons of uncertainty. We've become a culture of Prufrocks, T.S. Eliot's immortal whiner in "The Love Song of J. Alfred Prufrock"—

> *I grow old... I grow old...*
> *I shall wear the bottoms of my trousers rolled.*
> *Shall I part my hair behind? Do I dare to eat a peach?*
> *I shall wear white flannel trousers, and walk upon the beach.*
> *I have heard the mermaids singing, each to each.*
> *I do not think that they will sing to me.*[7]

No, the mermaids sing for no such man or woman. Crossing a continent on a bike is no heroic act of courage. Yet riders don't *expect* comfort, convenience, or security. What they do achieve, they carve out for themselves. If courage begins with facing life as it really is, then to ride is a first step. Best of all, if riding blasts us out of our dainty, Prufrock-like tremblings, then surely that's the start of overcoming—overcoming our fears, overcoming our inability to imagine a different life, overcoming our reluctance to venture things both great and small.

Ride. Just ride. And, as the wind rushes by, the mermaids *will* sing to you.

---

[7] T.S. Eliot, "The Love Song of J. Alfred Prufrock," *Collected Poems: 1909-1962* (Orlando, FL: Harcourt Brace & Company, 1963, 1991), p. 7.

Chapter 6:

Proud to Be an American

Monday, December 10
Ft. Stockton, TX to Sealy, TX—459 Miles

TRIP

The Trip:
Thanks, West Texas!

As often happens when riding, great days follow tough ones. After the challenges of last night—cold weather, finding gas, arriving too late to have dinner, not sleeping terribly well—Monday dawned sunny and bright.

Others who have made a long solo journey by motorcycle will understand the wonderful sense of solitude, the joy of devouring mile after mile, and the luxury of having plenty of time to think. So, in a sense, crossing America is a very solitary activity. Still, there are those special days when you realize that the experience is not only about the ride—but also very much about *people*.

After dining on peanuts and coffee last night, I was hungry this morning and looking forward to breakfast. I packed the bike before checking out, and set the alarm. Crossing the Swiss Clock Motel's parking lot, I purchased a newspaper and headed for the Alpine Lodge Restaurant's front door. Their outdoor *biergarten* looked pleasant. It was not hard to imagine sitting there on a warm summer night. Ft. Stockton looked a lot better by day than it had last night.

As I approached the restaurant door in my riding leathers, a rail-thin older man was leaving the restaurant. He paused, and held the door for me.

"Cold last night, weren't it, on that motorsicle?" he chuckled. I smiled and nodded agreement.

"I heerd you ride up. Yessir, I did. I heerd them pipes— 'durned' if I wouldn't do it myself, if I could. Well now, you have a good ride today." And with a big smile, he headed back to the lobby of the motel.

Alpine Lodge Restaurant, Ft. Stockton, TX

What a difference between *this* greeting and the suspicion that had greeted me at lunch in New Mexico. It wasn't that the people at lunch yesterday were unfriendly. They were just uninterested and wary of me—an outsider wearing odd clothes, traveling on a motorcycle. It was a pleasure this morning to be greeted cordially and have someone be interested in the trip.

The restaurant was comfortably warm without being stifling. Being from California, it's often hard to understand why people overheat and overcool buildings in most other parts of the country. Horticulturist Luther Burbank thought that Santa Rosa, California, was the most ideal climate in the world. That was why he based his life's work in Northern California—and as history demonstrates, he was recognized and visited in Santa Rosa by U. S. presidents, heads of state, and industry leaders for his accomplishments.

Whether Santa Rosa's climate is ideal or not, it does allow residents to live with their windows open, without heat or air conditioning, for most of the year. Even local stores and offices tend not to overheat or overcool. The contrast between the inside and outside temperatures is not as shocking (nor as unhealthy) as in much warmer or colder climates. Thankfully, the restaurant this morning was warm enough to be inviting but not so warm that I was too hot in my leathers.

Coffee arrived immediately, along with the cheery offer of a complete hot breakfast, all included in the room price. This made the Swiss Clock the deal-of-the-trip. For $45, not only had I enjoyed a large, clean room and bath, but also an ample supply of bacon, eggs, biscuits, and coffee. Breakfast was so enjoyable, I forgot to turn off the alarm before boarding the bike and alerted all of West Texas that Eli and I were about to depart. Didn't need loud pipes this morning.

The hospitality I enjoyed at the restaurant continued. West Texas was the best surprise of the trip. Most trips have such moments. During my August trip, Eastern Kansas was one such surprise. The soft summer evening air was so special, I stopped to stow all my riding gear, except T-shirt and jeans. I spent the rest of the daylight hours just cruising lazily along a mostly deserted Interstate, enjoying the smells and sensations of a late summer evening.

For different reasons, but with just as much pleasure, I savored the remainder of my ride from Ft. Stockton to Sealy, TX, in East Texas near Houston. Not only had people been pleasant at the Alpine Lodge Restaurant, but throughout the day Eli and I also encountered others who were interested and kind. While fueling in Sheffield, TX, under a giant Texas flag, my sunglasses fell off the top of a saddlebag when I turned Eli upright to begin fueling. A Softail can't be fully fueled on its sidestand, but must stand upright. The easiest way to do the job is to straddle the bike so its tanks are in the proper position. But now, perplexed by the prospect of losing my sunglasses, my only couse was to stop the pump, put Eli back on his sidestand, dismount, and retrieve my glasses—or risk having them lie on the pavement where any car passing close to the bike would crush them.

In less than the time it took me to decide, a man sitting in a wrecker on the other side of the filling station got out of his wrecker, crossed the station, picked up the glasses, and handed

Giant Texas flag and friendly folks, Sheffield, TX

them to me. I was astounded. Is this the self-centered 21st century? Not in Sheffield, TX! But that wasn't the end of it.

Shortly afterward, I stopped on the shoulder of I-10 to change gloves. I had pulled over for hardly 60 seconds when a stranger in a large, new pickup truck pulled in behind me. "Everything OK? I just saw you stop and wanted to be sure you were all right."

I would miss our home in Santa Rosa, if we were ever forced to leave for whatever reason. But if that were the case, "durned" if I wouldn't move to this part of Texas in a minute. As I continued eastward and passed Kerrville, I resolved to stop and spend more time here on the way back across the U.S.

Sealy was an undistinguished stop. Like many places when traveling far and fast, I'm sure I missed something good. But from the Holiday Inn Express, I walked to a Chinese restaurant located in a shopping center. It didn't look terribly interesting, despite a recommendation from the front desk. So, I wandered back through the dark parking lot, across a truck stop, and into a barbeque restaurant I'd spotted when exiting the highway. The food was so-so and the absence of table service made it even less appealing. Back at the Holiday Inn Express, I drifted off to sleep, looking forward to another day—and a better dinner—tomorrow.

Pre-Trip Preparation: Avoiding Boredom

PREP Non-riders sometimes get hung up about the amount of time alone riding long distances entails. Ron Ayres partially answers the question in his book *Against the Clock*, which chronicles his tour of 49 states in seven days:

> *We're frequently asked why riders participate in endurance events. What motivates us to ride so many miles in a day? What do we think about for all those*

hours? Isn't it totally boring? The implication is that being forced to be alone with one's thoughts for so long would be unpleasant.[1]

Ron's answers, I think, are fairly typical of any rider who wants to use his or her bike for serious travel. He points out that our bikes are comfortable, frequently more comfortable to us than traveling a similar distance in a car. This is certainly true in my case. In an automobile, I tend to get sleepy. On airline flights, I work or read. In both cases I end up shifting uncomfortably in my seat far more often than when settled behind the handlebars of my bike.

However, you may be wondering, "Can I really stand the potential boredom of crossing vast unpopulated distances?" I'll admit to a twinge of those feelings before my first trip. And although crossing Texas today completely dispelled whatever residual concerns I had about boredom, having some boredom avoidance techniques handy is valuable. Here are just a few ideas to file away before you leave home.[2]

Play mental games

For example, when on a potentially boring stretch of highway, where the distant horizon seems impossibly far away, guess the distance to the next curve or the next landmark. How far is it? Compare your guess to the actual distance measured on your odometer. Over time, you become good at visually estimating distances. You will also learn that our sense of scale performs quite differently in flat western terrain, compared with pine-tree lined Alabama highways.

---

[1] Ron Ayres, *Against the Clock* (North Conway, NH: Whitehorse Press, 1999), p. 13. This book, about the 1995 Iron Butt Rally, was written after *Against the Wind*.

[2] Jeff Galloway, in his book *Marathon: You Can Do It* writes at some length about techniques marathon runners can use to get through the difficult parts of a long race. The ideas presented here for riders have some of the same flavor.

Guess the distance to the horizon

Shift body and hand positions

Aside from shifting around on the seat to eliminate hot spots and discomfort, give your hands a break, too. Use your throttle locker or cruise control so that both your left *and* right hands get a break from constant contact with the handlebars. Find other comfortable positions for them.

At times, I simply rested my hands, one at a time. Other times, I used my resting hand to massage the top of my leg or a tight muscle in the opposite arm. At one point, I even played "airfoil" games. I found that by placing my right hand in a specific position on my right leg, I could completely eliminate all wind noise passing by my right ear. I could never get the same technique to work on the left side—nor could I make it work at all later in the trip. But a kind of childlike fascination with the fluid dynamics of airflow helped keep me alert and pass a couple of dozen miles at one point when I was beginning to feel some mental and physical fatigue.

Reflect on the differences between life on and off your bike

At one point during my journey, I realized that everything that felt right and worked well on the road—the extra long sleeves on my jacket, my Polartec neck protector, the full face helmet—all became uncomfortable or useless when I stopped. You can enrich your time on the road by thinking, "Why is this so?" and "What might this mean?"

For example, if the equipment and skills that are right and necessary on the road don't fit in my world off the bike, what extensions of that idea can I imagine? Could it be that strengths, which enabled me to overcome past challenges, might not help— or could even become uncomfortable—in the future? Draw analogies or create metaphors from riding and thinking in this way. You may find them useful later.

Just let your mind find its own course

Metaphorical reflection may be more than you want to tackle. During such times, of course, your mind must maintain two distinct streams of thought. You must maintain situational awareness—what's going on in front, beside, and behind your bike.

Mirror check. Peripheral scan. Eyes front. All's well.

But when riding, I tend to think "acceleratedly." Between the moments of absolute mental focus, which are required to remain safe, there is a more acute awareness of *everything*. Use that awareness to ponder the issues we push to the back of our minds. As our minds relax from the frantic pace maintained at home and at work, we can let them drift. Think of your wife or your husband; your fiancée; think of times with a good friend; your last holiday; a recipe you'd like to prepare when you get home (or better yet, for me at least, have prepared for you!).

You're alone, enjoying your ride. This time is all *yours!* These are only suggestions for passing the time, not an assignment. Susan and I have friends who operate a bed and breakfast in Colorado Springs. In each room, they have a sign that says:

Enjoy! This is not your mother's house.[3]

On the road, use your mental freedom creatively. And if that means not thinking of anything because you are constantly accountable for almost everything at home, then just relax. "Enjoy! This is not your mother's bike."

Your Equipment:
Deer Whistles

EQUIP

Riding last night, I worried about deer. Coming from a part of the country where these four-footed creatures are common, I consoled myself during the night that West Texas brush didn't provide enough nutrition to make it likely deer could survive there. The AAA materials described this stretch as "barren desert."

You can imagine my dismay, then, when one of the first road signs on leaving Ft. Stockton in the morning warned, "Beware of Deer." How many hours had I ridden in the dark last night, at freeway speeds, with no deer whistle and no special lighting? God be thanked for protecting children and those who sometimes don't use their good sense.

Knowing that injury and even death can result from a collision with a deer, I investigated deer whistles before leaving for the trip. It amazes me, of course, that a deer would not hear the pipes on most Harleys and run the other direction. A collision between two 700–800 pound contenders is going to leave both bloodied. But distance riders hit deer regularly. That had given me reason for concern prior to departure.

---

[3] Kaye and David Caster, The Old Town Guest House, Colorado Springs, CO. 888 375-4210 or *www.oldtown-guesthouse.com.*

Informed opinion seems to be on the side of riding with caution, because many deer whistles are of limited effectiveness. Their theory of operation is similar to a dog whistle. The whistle generates frequencies higher than we hear, but at sufficient intensity to attract the deer's attention and drive it from the road. There are a couple of caveats worth considering, however.

First, wind-driven whistles are useless at less than highway speeds because they depend on onrushing air to generate their sound. Yet, a collision with a deer is still a serious matter at almost any speed. Second, even the electronic whistles get mixed reports.[4] Some riders claim they are totally ineffective. Others feel they are better than nothing, but always ride with caution. I've met still other riders who hang a small bell or two from the bottom frame rail, believing that the high-pitched tinkle of the bell is about as effective as a deer whistle. One hopes so.

I wouldn't dismiss the effect of an electronic whistle, but your best defenses at night are speed management and good lighting. Speed management keeps you from over-riding your lights and being unable to stop if you suddenly encounter danger. Better lighting offers additional benefits beyond just helping you to spot wildlife sooner. You'll be safer throughout the night with a better view of the road. Higher intensity lighting also makes you more visible to other vehicles, during those hours when only your reflective gear and lights prevent nasty accidents.

Will better lighting and speed management absolutely prevent a collision with a deer? Sadly, no. Riders are hurt every year. Stay alert and be more cautious when riding on tree-lined roads or in other surroundings that allow deer to hide. And if the risk of traveling after dark is not necessary, consider just getting off the road and enjoy the pleasures of an early night.

---

[4] For an example of an electronic whistle, see *www.deer-whistles.com*.

RIDE

Riding Techniques: Pass Crushingly

Pass crushingly! If that sounds aggressive, it's not—but maybe the phrase will be memorable. That's the intent, because when you pass cars, as well as trucks that don't create turbulence, put down the hammer and get by as quickly as safety allows. Don't dawdle. That's what "pass crushingly" means.[5]

Your passes, whether on a freeway or a two-lane road, should be quick and clean. How often have you been frustrated behind a motorist who pulls into the left lane, but then dawdles along taking a minute or two to pass the vehicle in the right lane? Aside from tending to drive precise drivers and riders absolutely crazy, left-lane dawdlers endanger themselves and the vehicle they are passing. If an animal dashes in front of the car in the right lane, or a motorist on the shoulder suddenly decides to re-enter traffic, the natural reaction of the car being passed is to swerve into the passing lane. So, get past! The fewer seconds you allow another vehicle inside your bubble, the safer you'll be.

Bikers need to be even more careful than motorists. Passing has three phases, the "Three Ps:"

Phase I: Planning

Look well ahead and determine how you'll escape, should the worst happen. A swerve, a tire exploding, an unexpected piece of debris in the road, and more can force the worst upon you. Normally your escape route is along the left shoulder. Even on urban freeways, there is typically enough room between the leftmost lane and the retaining wall or center guardrail to allow a motorcycle to pass.

---

[5] For a discussion of truck-passing techniques, see Chapter 5.

Phase II: Passing

With your escape route planned, roll on sufficient power to eclipse the speed of the vehicle you are passing. Your objective is not to terrify the occupants by passing like a rocket, but you want to minimize the time spent beside them or in their mirrors' blind spots. Make your pass in one, smooth sweep that begins at least a couple of seconds behind the vehicle (remember MSF's "one thousand one, one thousand two"). Don't wait until you are within a car length or two of the vehicle in front of you.

Phase III: Positioning

After you've gotten past the vehicle to your right, don't be in a hurry to return to the right lane. Do a mirror check and a head check. Glance briefly over your right shoulder to confirm the information gathered from your mirror. Even then, consider giving yourself another couple of seconds before you signal and pull back into the right lane. By this time you should be in a position more than two seconds ahead of whatever you passed.

One more thought: some of us believe that loud pipes save lives. Anything that alerts other motorists to our presence may help avoid the cry heard so often after fatal car/motorcycle collisions, "I never saw him!"

If you do have loud pipes, however, build up enough speed so that you can throttle back *just slightly* as you go by the vehicle you are passing. Don't roll off to the degree recommended in Chapter 5 for loading the front fork when passing a truck. Roll off just enough so your engine purrs. While the benefit of your pipes is that the drivers of adjacent vehicles almost certainly know you are nearby, the downside of open pipes at full throttle is they can be genuinely startling—even when your pass was expected. Be courteous and avoid a potentially unsafe situation. Roll off slightly, particularly if the driver's side window is open.

And give the driver a wave and a smile as you pass. Every friend we make for motorcycling is worthwhile.

Thoughts from the Road:
May We Never Forget

When we ride, we have time to ponder life's dilemmas. We won't solve all the world's problems. But sometimes we go home with more perspective.

It was impossible, riding only months after 9/11, to cross America without thinking of the horrible tragedy that struck our country. Terrorists used civilian airliners to attack civilian targets. No airman who has ever been responsible for the lives of others would ever allow an intruder to fly his or her aircraft into a building. We owe those aircrews the same respect as the other heroes of 9/11. On the day of the attack, if the U.S. military had asked all pilots to attack Al Qaeda targets, I'd have been first in line to volunteer. But our country has better men, flying better equipment.

I write that to make it clear what follows in no way supports any sick terrorist's aims. However, what concerned me as I rode today is that many allies in Europe and Asia complain the way of life America exports is not always admirable. Maybe these thoughts came to mind today because I met so many wonderful Americans: the man at the Alpine Lodge Restaurant, the wrecker operator who picked up my sunglasses, the pickup driver who stopped to be sure I was OK. But it's not hard to see worrisome examples of who we are, as well.

Have we become blind to the offensive image exported through much of today's American music and too many Hollywood films? Is there a degree to which the world is right, when they label our pop culture a virus? That's sad, because there is so much is good, noble, right, courageous, and generous about American people.

May we show the world who we really are—not the villains a small group of depraved hijackers claim we are. May we maintain the unity that galvanized the U.S. immediately after the World Trade Center and Pentagon attacks. May we applaud and support police and fire personnel everywhere in America, just as we did in Manhattan after the attacks. May we remember the U.S. military personnel who serve daily in over 100 countries so that we can ride free and live in safety. May we give them the funds and the tools they need to do their jobs well. May each of us bear our responsibility for preserving and enhancing liberty and justice for all. And, despite our shortcomings, may we realize all the benefits we enjoy as Americans, from the poorest to the wealthiest.

And may we never, ever forget.

Chapter 7:

Louisiana 1927

Tuesday, December 11
Sealy, TX to Biloxi, MS—463 Miles

The Trip:
Laid Back in Louisiana

When I awoke in Sealy, the air didn't smell different, not yet—but I knew it would before the day was over. With any progress, I should see Biloxi by nightfall and Greenville, SC, the following evening. Between here and South Carolina, breathing some moist, Gulf air was a welcome thought.

In contrast to West Texas, East Texas turned out to be the least pleasant part of the trip so far. Leaving Sealy, Houston was the next major city. By the time I reached Houston, a drizzle had begun. The traffic was so heavy I decided to bypass the city on the ring road, Highway 8, the Sam Houston Parkway. Highway 8 is a toll road. While it was a relief to be moving rather than sitting in traffic, the tollbooths seemed only minutes apart. Each of them was increasingly difficult to manage—finding money and stowing receipts—in gloves, rain gear, and the drizzle that had become a downpour. Oil slicks at each stop added to the tension. I was thankful for one woman toll-taker who saw the oil, the rain, and my bike, and said, "Be careful."

Getting out of Texas at midday was wonderful. Apologies to the Bush family, who have ties to Houston and Beaumont. It was a relief to enter laid-back Louisiana. Even the weather improved, with the rain stopping.

Despite Louisiana's reputation for difficult-to-pronounce French and Cajun place names, I found the signs charming. For example, it was handy to see a place called "Iota." If you decided to stay for the night, you could tell people you weren't "going one Iota farther!" Similarly, the exit for "Cecilia Henderson" was intriguing. What did she do to rate her own highway sign? I wanted to meet her, just to find out. Down the road a bit was "Baptist Pumpkin Center." Having only known Presbyterian and Lutheran pumpkins, the Baptist Pumpkin Center interested me, too—but, alas, there was no time.

Stopping near Evangeline allowed me to pay tribute to the survivors of the 1927 flood, immortalized in Randy Newman's song. The stop coincided with Eli's need for gas and mine for a break. This mini-mart also offered the trip's most unusual gift item—dried alligator heads in a variety of sizes.

Louisiana offered more than interesting place names and alligator heads for gifts, however. Henderson Swamp is genuinely impressive. Apparently the swamp is so impenetrable that the entire region is bridged with a structure much like the Seven Mile Bridge in the Florida Keys. Eli and I were suspended above the marshy land for mile after mile. It wasn't difficult to imagine how someone could simply disappear into the swamp in a flat-bottomed boat—never again to be found by the less venturesome. Are there houses on poles with boats docked underneath? Maybe real privacy, even isolation, would be possible here. As day turned to dusk and then dark, the water in the moonlight beneath the bridge turned milky white. It looked like a snowscape. Only trees rose from the ghostly whiteness. Once again I was thankful for Eli's incredible reliability. This was not a place I'd be eager to be stranded.

It was after dark when Eli and I reached Biloxi. I had expected the town to be along I-10, so it took a bit of exploration to find I-110 and the center of town. My Dad served in the military in Biloxi during the 1940s. Since then, it has become Atlantic City South or Las Vegas East. Casinos dominate the landscape. Having seen billboard upon billboard for cheap rooms, I phoned to be sure they weren't full. They were not and a gorgeous room at The Grand Casino was only $39. Eating dinner anywhere in the hotel, however (and there were precious few choices outside the hotel), more than offset any savings on the room.

Tired and frustrated by the long day, the difficulty in finding Biloxi, and the false economy of the room price, I retired. Still, I was ready for the final push to Greenville. Only "one more sleep" as my daughter and I often say when counting down days before a visit or other important event.

Pre-Trip Preparation: Protect Your Tools

PREP Riding in a steady drizzle part of today made me realize I'd forgotten to protect my tool kit. Depending on where you carry your tools, your situation may not demand bagging items in your kit in plastic. But on the Softail, I use a leather bag hung from the lowest point of the frame, just ahead of the engine. This location keeps its weight and the bike's center of gravity low. But, it also puts the bag in a continuous stream of water spinning up from the front tire.

Thankfully, good tools (good quality socket wrenches, screwdrivers, crescent wrenches, and so on) probably won't require special treatment. Their plating or the base metal from which they are made makes them corrosion resistant. However, other tools and supplies aren't designed to take such abuse. When I reached Greenville and checked the kit, my Allen wrenches, some of the Torx keys, and a couple of other items I'd thrown into the kit had all rusted. Cleaning them up was an unexpected chore.

Eli's low hanging toolkit gets wet in the rain

Don't make my mistake. Protect your tools before departing. Enclose vulnerable tools and supplies in Ziploc plastic bags. If your tools are in a pouch, place that in a larger plastic bag. When you arrive at your destination, inspect your kit and let it dry out thoroughly. You don't want to need a tool along the way just to discover it is rusted or ruined.

Your Equipment: Eating En Route

EQUIP Road food. After water, the second most important thing your body needs is food. We discussed getting enough water (and getting rid of it) in Chapter 5; now let's talk about food.

Ron Ayres visited 49 states in seven days, missing only Hawaii, by eating mostly bananas. He became well known for this food preference, to the point that well-wishers greeted him at stops with fresh bananas! [1] While bananas worked for Ron, most of us require heartier fare, particularly if we aren't riding to set a record and can set aside a little more time to eat.

When you're touring on your bike, you can take time to stop and enjoy leisurely meals. As a friend of mine wrote, after he read an early draft of this book:

> *Distance per time is not my forte. I've ridden about 175,000 miles on a bike but never more than 600-700 in a day. I prefer 300 miles/day with four beer stops, one fishing stop, one billiards stop, one swim stop, and one hike/walk/site-checkout stop. When I was a bit younger, we (10 to 15 guys) would take two weeks, usually with no destination and definitely no route. The first day would be five to seven beer stops and about 50 miles, then we'd settle in to 200-300 a day.* [2]

When riding to a destination, nevertheless, your time and food options may be much more limited.

Your tastes and metabolism tell you what works best for you. Mini-marts are a boon to distance riders, because you can stop and eat something quickly—ideally something healthier than the

---

[1] Ayres, *Against the Clock.*
[2] Wayne "Trees" Simoni, email, January 26, 2002.

typical fast-food meal. During my August trip across the country, I would look for a gas station with a mini-mart for breakfast. A container of cottage cheese or yogurt, a cup of coffee, and a multivitamin suited me perfectly. But you may prefer to start the day with a bigger, hot breakfast before leaving your motel. Not all motels offer hot breakfasts, so if you require such a meal, pick your stopping places accordingly.

During the day your options narrow even further. What you eat becomes a function of how far you want to travel, although none of us should skip food entirely during regular mealtimes. You may find you are satisfied with a quick burger or a microwave sandwich. But even on my 1,099-mile day during the return trip (from Greenville, SC to just short of San Antonio, TX; see Chapter 9), I stopped for one hot meal. Without it I don't think I'd have had the endurance to complete the distance.

Some road food is better than other road food

When you eat matters almost as much as *what* you eat. Endurance athletes learn to eat before they "bonk"—before they run out of energy. Long distance riders should do the same thing. It is a much better strategy to eat something frequently than to ride most of the day and try to make up for missed meals at dinner. While dinner may be enjoyable, you risk low blood sugar during the day and allowing your alertness to wane. You should also carry along some energy bars or other healthy snack food just in case a restaurant or mini-mart isn't available. The night I had to eat peanuts from the motel vending machine, I was wishing I'd remembered to pack some Clif Bars.

One final note about food. In his book *The Zone*, Dr. Barry Sears makes the point that food is a drug—a powerful drug.[3] We don't often think of meals in that way. And compared to powerful therapeutic drugs, of course, the effect of what we eat is much more subtle. Still, too much sugar leads to energy followed by fatigue; too much caffeine can do the same and prompt an upset stomach, too. You should think of food as riding equipment, the same way you think about gloves or a jacket or boots. No one diet suits every rider, but take time to think about your food, before you depart and during each day. You'll be a better, safer, and happier rider as a result.

Riding Techniques: Anticipation and Looking Ahead

RIDE

Chapter 5 talked about maintaining a bubble around your bike, just like air traffic controllers maintain separation both vertically and laterally between aircraft. How do we, as riders, create and maintain that same kind of bubble?

---

[3] Barry Sears, *The Zone* (New York: HarperCollins, 1995).

"Well, we just do it," you might reply—and we do. But identifying the underlying skills that actually *enable* us to do it may help us do it better, more consistently, and thus, more safely.

Maintaining your bubble

The key skill in maintaining your bubble is *anticipation*. Riders must constantly monitor vehicle mix, traffic vectors, and road speeds. For example, one-half mile ahead, you spot a slow moving truck in the right lane. This tells the experienced rider that cars behind it are going to veer into the left lane to pass. If you are riding in the left lane, you should anticipate the movement of conflicting traffic into your lane, to maintain separation and safety.

But how do you anticipate traffic movements under less predictable circumstances or when faced with erratic drivers? What can we do to hone our anticipation skills and increase the margin of safety?

Look farther ahead.   Many riders look only two to three seconds ahead. A longer view—10, 15, even 20–30 seconds—translates into much more time and distance to make adjustments to your course and speed. Look at the distances in the following table.

| Speed (mph) | Distance in Feet, Traveled in Seconds | | | | | |
	1 sec	2 sec	3 sec	5 sec	10 sec	15 sec
30	44	88	132	220	440	660
40	58	116	172	290	580	870
50	73	146	219	365	730	1,095
60	88	176	264	440	880	1,320
70	102	204	306	510	1,020	1,530
80	117	234	351	585	1,170	1,755
90	132	264	396	660	1,320	1,980

Using the table, let's work through an example. At 70 mph freeway speeds and looking only one second ahead, you have 102 feet—about 30 yards—to adjust your course or speed. Sound like a lot of space? Remember, you have to recognize the situation and respond in one second. Reaction times can be longer than that. At the same speed, but looking *five* seconds ahead, you have 510 feet—almost the length of two football fields—to respond and adjust. If you're good and traffic permits, look 15 seconds ahead. You will have more than a quarter mile to blend your course with others or to avoid unanticipated hazards.

I don't know about you, but I'd much rather have the safety that goes with larger amounts of time and distance. Be thankful we don't share the challenges faced by Concorde pilots: they travel a full mile every 2.6 seconds!

How do we gain that distance and time? First, break old habits and train yourself to look and think farther ahead. Where we look is more a matter of habit than training. For example, marathon runners sometimes let their heads drop and look only a dozen or so steps ahead—staring at the road or trail. By lifting their heads, they improve their form *and* get a better view of the competition/traffic. At the beginning of a marathon with thousands of runners, there can be more traffic per square foot of roadway than we will ever face on a freeway—even during rush hour. So, look up; look ahead of your bike.

Start by scanning out away from your bike, and then scanning back. Some riders find it uncomfortable to constantly keep their focus 10–15 seconds ahead of the bike. Pavement conditions or debris in the road are concerns. By scanning out and back, you cover threats near and far. Think like a windshield wiper, but a windshield wiper lying on the pavement, swinging out and back rather than side-to-side.

Use lane position.   Once you're looking and thinking farther ahead, start using lane position to your advantage. Unless I'm in merging traffic, I ride on the right-hand side of the *right* lane or the left-hand side of the *left* lane. This keeps me closer to the best escape routes if something goes awry in front of me. However, if freeway traffic is especially heavy and slow, I often ride very close to the stripe that divides the lanes (that is, near the left-hand edge of the *right* lane; near the right-hand edge of the *left* lane). Doing so allows me to look farther ahead and between the lanes of traffic for clues about sudden stops, drivers changing lanes, or a tailgater rear-ending the vehicle ahead of him/her.

Automobile drivers don't have this luxury. They can't choose a lane position. They might shift their car a few feet either way, but because of their left-hand driving position, their sightline in either lane is relatively fixed. As a motorcyclist, you can move around strategically to provide the best possible view of what is ahead. Use that difference to your advantage. Sometimes we fall into old habits of riding like we drive. Check yourself the next time you are on a freeway to see if you're inadvertently doing the same thing.

Even with a bubble, always have an escape route

Finally, let me emphasize again the importance of escape routes— know where you'll go in case of trouble! Try to have two or three possible escapes. On freeways, the right or left shoulder usually is first choice. Avoid riding in center lanes for this reason. In addition to subjecting yourself to threats from both sides, you have no certain escape like the shoulder, which is almost always clear.

You can create additional escape routes by maintaining your bubble and having good situational awareness.

Consider this example. You are riding in the left lane of a four-lane freeway—two lanes each direction, with a barrier between you and the traffic coming from the opposite direction.

A driver five cars ahead of you suddenly brakes to avoid a large piece of tractor-trailer tire tread in his lane. The tailgater behind that car doesn't notice until too late. The collision of those two cars causes the remaining three cars to dive toward the left shoulder—hoping to thread the needle between the accident and the retaining wall between your side of the freeway. But one of the drivers was not sufficiently skillful to accomplish that maneuver and crashes into the concrete barrier. The shoulder is now blocked. Where do you go?

You've been riding skillfully, maintaining separation of at least two to three seconds behind the car immediately in front of you. You have also been scanning your mirrors, with careful attention to the right lane. As a result, you not only know that you have sufficient space ahead of your bike, but you also know the lane is clear immediately to your right. When the accident occurs, you simply move right and reassess the situation from a place that offers at least two options: slowing down, but continuing in the right-hand lane, or going all the way through the right-hand lane and onto the right shoulder.

Either way, of course, if you had a clear view of the accident, you must stop, assist any injured, and be available to make a police report. But because of your riding strategy, you are a witness to this accident, not a part of it.

Staying Organized: Restroom Stops

I never thought that, at my age and with grown children, I'd seek out restrooms with baby changing stations. However, it doesn't take long to discover that most public restrooms aren't made for motorcyclists. Helmets and gloves alone present a challenge when you're squeezing into cramped toilets or standing at a urinal. If you're carrying a shoulder bag or anything else that has to be parked while using the facilities, limited space and missing door hooks make rest stops tough. As a result, the increasing availability of fold-down changing tables may be the most important contribution of the last 10–15 years' trend toward equal opportunity diaper changing.

Even with the convenience of changing tables, remember to do two things as you leave the restroom:

- Pay attention to sequence
- Scan the area carefully

Despite my best efforts to make organized, quick stops, early in the trip I tended to forget the sequence for putting back on all my gear. I would have to remove my helmet again because I'd forgotten to reinsert my earplugs. Or I'd have to take off my leather jacket because I'd forgotten to hold the power cords for my electric gloves—resulting in the cords being lost somewhere in my sleeves. Think sequence. Your stops will be better organized and quicker as a result.

Learn to scan any area you leave. More than once I left something behind on a door hook or elsewhere, from scattering things too widely during my stops. This problem is more likely during a winter trip, when you are wearing a lot of clothing. You may put your helmet in one place, hang your jacket in another, and so on. Don't, if you can avoid it. Fold-up baby changing tables make a wonderful platform to keep all your gear clean, well organized, and high above (hmm, what shall we say?) less than perfectly sanitary floors.

Thoughts from the Road: Imagine a Different Life

POST

I thought more about Ben and Elinore Carlin as I crossed into the southeastern U.S. today. Nothing in my journey approached the risk of an ocean passage in a Jeep. Yet maybe their voyage and mine shared a similar motivation. "Cutting yourself free from the ridiculous trappings and entanglements of civilized existence,"[4] is how Ben put it.

We don't think much about our entanglements. We should. Certainly the biggest entanglement for most of us is our job. While the demands of farming are not easy, the pace is human and partly self-determined. This was even truer in the past. Life on the farm was attuned to the seasons. In temperate climates, the seasons themselves prompted occasions for rest. The idea of stopping work for a while, in order to return to work refreshed and productive, was built into the work itself.[5] But as the industrial revolution began and scientific management gained favor, other priorities emerged. For example, in a 1914 debate with Frederick Taylor, the father of scientific management, a machinist argued:

> *We don't want to work as fast as we are able to. We want to work as fast as we think it's comfortable for us to work. We haven't come into existence for the purpose of seeing how great a task we can perform through a lifetime. We are trying to regulate our work so as to make it auxiliary to our lives.*[6]

As I rode, I thought about how little we seem to have learned. "Maximize shareholder value" and "beat the estimates of The Street" are only the latest expressions of what that machinist feared in 1914. And today, many of us also work to pay for self-inflicted

---

[4] Ben Carlin, *Half Safe*, p. 47.

[5] Shoshanna Zuboff, *In the Age of the Smart Machine: The Future of Work and Power* (New York: Basic Books, Inc., 1988). Zuboff's book is largely about the application of technology to our work. But her first three chapters, including "The Laboring Body: Suffering and Skill in Production Work," "The Abstraction of Industrial Work," and "The White-Collar Body in History" are worth reading—even if you have no interest in computer technology.

[6] Quoted by Zuboff, p. 46.

trappings: the big house, SUVs and Mercedes, lavish vacations, and therapists.

Does two weeks really amount to a "vacation," especially if you have to work so hard you can't take it—or can't take two weeks all at once? Europeans recognize that a true holiday requires time to unwind. Many of them spend as much as four to six weeks away from work each year. Few companies in the U.S. even offer four to six weeks of vacation or extended-leave sabbaticals. And even fewer of us would have the length of service usually needed to qualify. What has happened to our notion of rest? Of Sabbath? Of holiday? Of regulating our work, rather than our work regulating us?

As I rode through city after city, past office building after office building, I thought about these things. Do we even think about freedom? Do we consider cutting free? As Zuboff wrote of the workers at one pulp and paper mill, "It was not that they wanted to work as hard as they did but that they never seriously considered any alternative."[7]

Imagine life! Alternatives exist. The road is there. As I stood in the fresh air and Louisiana sunshine, enjoying a break and admiring Eli's muscular engine and glossy flanks, I smiled and thought, "We're free, my friend. If only for a short time, we're free."

---

[7] Zuboff, p. 91.

Chapter 8:

Lost Highway
Wednesday, December 12
Biloxi, MS to Greenville, SC—534 Miles

TRIP

The Trip:
Arrival!
Propping myself up in bed at The Grand Casino in Biloxi, the panoramic view from my room made it clear today's weather could be a problem. Except for the sand storm between Indio and Blythe and a little rain yesterday, I'd had great weather for the ride. But outside the glass separating my air-conditioned room from the moist Gulf air, clouds were rising. Cumulus clouds build from hot air and moisture. How long would it be before that moisture fell today?

Once outside, I thought about riding without a jacket, just for the breeze. But the forecast said severe storms throughout the Mississippi River valley, with the weather clearing east of Mobile, AL. Opened the zippered vents in my leather jacket. If the weather deteriorated, I would stop and put on my rain suit.

One of the primary sources of entertainment while riding after dark yesterday was the sweeping expanse of casino advertisements. Each brightly lit billboard offered more slots, cheaper rooms, better food, or bigger-name entertainers. Having sworn off Las Vegas long ago (which is a lot closer to home), I didn't have any special hankering for gambling or shows. But the prospect of a deluxe $39 room had been too good to pass up.

A vague theory formed in my mind as I carried my luggage through the lobby toward the bike. Casinos must be one answer to loneliness. They are bright, not dark. People are around; you are never alone. Casinos are open 24 hours; if you can't sleep, they offer something to do.

My own momentary loneliness on this trip had caused me to bunk in a casino last night. I wanted to be in a place where the door of my room opened to something more than the dark outside and an empty bed within. Does loneliness or fear of death perhaps contribute to the popularity of casinos—particularly among so many seniors I saw wandering the halls? Dylan Thomas wrote:

Do not go gentle into that good night,
Old age should burn and rave at the close of day;
Rage, rage against the dying of the light.[1]

I couldn't think of any other reason why men and women, grandmothers and grandfathers, even friends and neighbors would stroll among garish slots or stare distractedly at lounge entertainers. After one night, I was ready for my self-imposed aloneness again.

Not far from the Alabama-Mississippi state line, the clouds grew darker and I stopped to change into rain gear. As I entered the mini-mart, I saw a line near the men's room. But folks weren't waiting for the restrooms. They were lined up for Miss Nikki's freshly cooked sausage biscuits. Miss Nikki, proprietress, had come from the Chalkidiki region—the hand-and-fingers shaped part of

---

[1] Dylan Thomas, "Do Not Go Gentle into that Good Night," *The Poems of Dylan Thomas*, published by New Directions. Copyright © 1952, 1953 Dylan Thomas. Copyright © 1937, 1945, 1955, 1962, 1966, 1967 the Trustees for the Copyrights of Dylan Thomas. Copyright © 1938, 1939, 1943, 1946, 1971 New Directions Publishing Corp.

Greece—to see the 1964 World's Fair in New York. Far from home, she figured she might as well visit family in Canada and Kansas City, too. As things go, she met her future husband in Kansas City, married, and remained in the U.S. "Do you miss Greece?" I asked. "Yes, at Christmas, very much" she smiled. "There is much more emphasis on family and baking there—much less on gifts and spending."

Not only did she have her priorities straight, but her sausage biscuits were better than good. I left reluctantly, but hoped to make Greenville without another overnight, if possible. Only 533 miles separate Biloxi and Greenville. Should be doable. Might even be easy.

As the miles clicked by, smells returned. I'd missed them! On my August trip, I had inhaled America: redwoods and eucalyptus in California, the hot desert air in Nevada, freshly mown grass in Kansas, the soft evening air in the South, garlic from kitchens and restaurants. Suddenly, today, the aromas of America returned. The moist Gulf air; pine forests; pungent red earth exposed by bulldozers working next to the highway; warm, clean horses in the open trailer ahead of me; mouth watering, hickory-smoked barbeque from a roadside stand. I was happy again.

Louisiana's charming road signs spilled over into Mississippi and Alabama. "Georgianna Starlington" earned an exit sign on I-65 in Alabama. Who was this lovely belle? I'd known no Georgianna Starlington while I was growing up. There was no time to stop. One could imagine a sweeping drama, akin to *Gone With the Wind*, which inspired such a name. Maybe it helped that her exit was on the "Hank Williams Lost Highway." What plot, what tragedy, waiting to be written!

I pulled into a station for gas. The informal mayor of the station and assorted friends ambled over to take a look.

"Trade you a '64 Ford for that thang," he smiled.

Eli relaxing for a minute—one more gas stop

"No thanks. I might miss it," I answered. And I would. Thankfully, Eli is occasionally willing to suffer being genderless in some conversations, for the sake of not setting off alarms with people who might not understand "miss him."

A couple more interested bystanders walked up. One had lived in Rock Hill, SC, not far from where I was headed. The other worked in Mississippi, but was heading to Mobile, AL, to be with his kids for Christmas. I told him I was heading to South Carolina to do the same thing.

"You don't live with them?" he prodded.

"No, they're 30 and 28."

"Aw, shoot. I thought you was a *young* man!" he replied. Best compliment I'd had all day.

Ride on. Passing from Alabama into Georgia, traffic slowed noticeably. I don't know if this resulted from some lack of regard for the Alabama State Police (I saw no evidence why this should be so) or whether I'd just entered a particularly well-patrolled part of

Georgia. I rolled off the power and fell in behind the traffic cruising at or below the limit.

While stopped at the La Grange Travel Center, not far across the Georgia line, rain finally began to fall. This was not good, given that I'd arrive in Atlanta after dark during rush hour. As a result of the city's growth spurt in the 1980s and the 1996 Summer Olympics, Atlanta's freeways are good. But the sheer sprawl of the city has never been easy to negotiate. I wasn't looking forward to the combination of rain, darkness, and thousands of impatient and tired commuters.

Phoned family. Updated my estimated time of arrival. Now what? Same answer as 2,714 miles ago. Just ride. Get on the bike and put in the mileage. I really didn't want to stop overnight so close to the end.

But, "so close" can be measured many ways. In statute miles, I was close at less than 200 miles. On the other hand, measured by the dangers of riding amidst work-crazed drivers paying no attention to a tired Harley rider, I was still far from my destination. The hour spent crossing Atlanta was among the worst of the trip. It rivaled St. Louis in the rain during August. Like any good, defensive rider, I try to make myself visible and audible to the vehicles around me. A porcupine strategy, being prickly, keeps drivers aware of you—whether through loud pipes, frequent hand signals, flashing lights, or movement to maintain separation.

But tonight, nothing worked. From minivans to Porsches, the traffic was horrible. Finally, in the heart of Atlanta, a particularly indifferent driver forced me off the freeway onto an exit ramp leading to Heaven-only-knows where. Atlanta's freeways have a peculiar design. Their right lanes transform themselves into exits much more frequently than in other cities. Who knows? It may be the only way to get the city's residents off the freeways. Right now, however, it means I'm getting a tour of the belly of the beast.

Having read that Atlanta's crime rate is second only to Detroit, let's hope the image of Harley riders as people not to be messed with serves me well through the city.

I made my way back to the freeway, and an hour or so later, crossed into South Carolina on I-85. The fifth state in one day— what a difference from the trip's start when one state took two days to cover. Even better, the goal for the day was clearly in sight.

Finally, arrival! Pulling into Greenville offered a much-welcomed haven. I'd made it. My daughter, Mercedes, and her husband, Doug, met me in the driveway of their home. Their enthusiastic greetings and the knowledge that I'd soon be enjoying a good meal—despite the late hour—made getting off the bike easier. As I removed the saddlebags and shouldered my Lazy Rider bag, I could feel the tensions of Atlanta at rush hour easing. I gently ran a hand over Eli's tank, to let him know how much I appreciated his reliability, his faithfulness in every climate, every situation.

"Goodnight, Eli. Rest well. You've earned it, my friend."

Atlanta had battered, but not beaten us. Eli and I were here. Half the journey was complete!

Reviewing the trip at the halfway mark

Pre-Trip Preparation: Avoiding Get-There-Itis

PREP

A lot of important pre-trip preparation occurs each day of the trip before leaving the motel—not months before you leave home. Today I failed to do my daily pre-trip planning and ended up in Atlanta at the worst possible time.

Recognize the warning signs

No schedule is worth risking your life. Watch for the deadly symptoms of "get-there-itis." This disease strikes when you are close to your destination. Your desire to get there overrides your good judgment about the risks. Unnecessary pressures you put on yourself or others put on you can exacerbate get-there-itis. The same potentially deadly disease affects motorists, boaters, private pilots—all of us.

"Oh, you aren't going to let a little storm keep you from departing, are you?"

"We need to get home! Can't we leave now?"

"If we don't get there tomorrow, the deal we've worked on for months is going to fall apart. You don't want that, do you?"

The right question is, "What is your life worth?" No schedule, no desire to get there, no deal is worth your life. In retrospect, as much as I wanted to be in Greenville with my family, I should have stopped prior to Atlanta for dinner and allowed the traffic to clear. Or, I could have checked into a motel and made an easy ride to Greenville the next day. But I did what I should not have done. I put myself at risk by competing for drivers' attention in darkness and rain, at the peak of rush hour.

Even Iron Butt competitors, who rack up incredibly long distances each day during the rally, know when to stop. Among the 29 tips in the Archive of Wisdom on the Iron Butt Association web site is, "Learn to stop, to go faster."[2] Watch yourself. Get-there-itis is deadly.

The desire to make a round trip when you don't have enough time is another time to beware of get-there-itis. This happened during my August trip. As mentioned in the Preface, work forced me to return home sooner than I'd expected. I could have attempted several long-distance days, but opted to ship the bike home and fly back instead.

Have a contingency plan (you may need to ship the bike)

Be ready, if get-there-it is attacks you. Have a contingency plan in mind in case a family emergency occurs, problems erupt at work, or you no longer feel you can complete the trip safely.

Shipping firms can pick up your motorcycle almost anywhere and deliver it cross-country, sometimes in a matter of days. I used Harley Transport, but their services aren't limited to Harley-Davidsons. In fact, their new web site is *www.MotorcycleShipping.biz*. After searching the Web and calling around, I found these folks to be incredibly friendly and helpful. Other shippers are listed in the Supplier's Guide at the end of this book.

If you decide to ship your bike, be sure to ask the right questions.

How much insurance is included in the standard shipping rate and is extra available? For my Harley, some companies couldn't cover replacement value with all its modifications and accessories. They responded that my regular motorcycle insurance should cover any loss—so their coverage was supplemental—but be sure you *know* your bike is fully insured by someone before you ship.

---

[2] Go to *www.ironbutt.com* and click "Archive of Wisdom."

Will you be charged extra for a residential pick-up or delivery?
Don't be surprised if the answer is "yes." If you think about it, it
makes sense. Your bike is going to be loaded on a semi that can't
be parked easily on some residential roads (can't even maneuver
on some of them). If you can arrange to have your bike shipped
dealer to dealer, you'll probably get better pricing—and you'll have
someone at each end to drain or refill the gas tank, disconnect or
connect the battery, and more. I shipped from Harley-Davidson of
Greenville,[3] where Wyatt Wilson and his team were happy to prep
the bike for shipment and hold it until the truck arrived. Michael's
Harley-Davidson in Cotati, California, where the bike is usually
serviced, were equally happy to receive it and check it out after
the shipping. You should expect to pay for this service, but if the
dealer refuses payment, drop off a case of good beer or give your
contact a twenty-dollar bill—so he or she can thank the tech(s)
who prep your bike.

When will the bike be loaded and when will it arrive?   These
questions are obvious, but by asking, you sometimes uncover
helpful options. When I talked with Harley Transport by phone,
it turned out that if I were willing to drop off the bike at H-D of
Greenville only a couple of days earlier than I'd planned, it would
arrive in California almost 10 days earlier than the next-best arrival
date. Shipping companies generally wait for a full load before
starting, so be flexible on timing. Ask around to see if you can get
your bike on a truck that arrives as close to your desired delivery
date as possible.

You may be concerned about the cost of shipping your bike
and returning home by air. For me, the shipping cost about equaled
expected food, gas, and lodging costs for the return trip. So, the

---

[3] See *www.h-dog.com.*

shipping was a wash. My daughter and her husband generously donated airline miles for me to fly home. That may not be possible in your situation, but something to keep in mind if you have get home quickly. In the end, if this money helps you avoid the risks of get-there-itis, it is money well spent.

Your Equipment: Nighttime Visibility

EQUIP

Tonight's experience in Atlanta underscored the importance of rain and night-riding accessories. If the most common lament of automobile drivers after colliding with a motorcycle is "I never saw him," then we owe it to ourselves to be extraordinarily visible.

Review your clothing, your luggage, and your bike, asking yourself the following questions.

Does my rain gear have adequate reflective material located in a variety of places?

It does you no good at night or in a rainstorm, if your rain suit or jacket has only a reflective stripe across its back, hidden by the luggage stacked behind you.

Be certain your suit has reflective material on the chest, back, sleeves, and legs. One of those areas should be always visible. It is also helpful to have reflective material on your gloves. At times I found myself signaling cars using old-fashioned hand signals— because the likelihood of them noticing the motion of the bright reflective stripe on my glove seemed more probable than simply using the bike's turn signals.

You may also want to consider getting a runner's reflective vest much like school crossing guards wear (but lighter weight). Placing the vest over your jacket at night, during dry rides, will make you more visible.

Reflective material on jacket keeps you visible

Does my helmet have either reflective tape or reflective stickers to attract attention at night?

Manufacturers sometimes caution users about mounting stickers or decals on their helmets, for fear of compromising the strength of the shell. But post-Atlanta, I find that risk less compelling than remaining visible under all conditions. I had an AMA (American Motorcyclist Association) sticker on the back of my full-face helmet, just above the Shoei logo. Riding through Atlanta in the dark and rain at rush hour, I wished I had also affixed reflective tape to the helmet.[4]

---

[4] See Whitehorse Press, either their web site (*www.whitehorsepress.com*) or print catalog. They offer a variety of reflective stick-on materials to augment your visibility.

Does my luggage have reflective material?

Some manufacturers sew reflective piping or other material into soft luggage. If you have a hard trunk on your bike, it probably also has some reflective gear. Adding reflective tape or rear-facing red lights to your luggage increases the outline of your visibility to drivers around you. Permanently mounted luggage can take hardwired lights. For soft luggage, clip on a couple of battery-powered flashing lights used by bicyclists or reflective patches used by runners. [5]

Does my bike have adequate night lighting?

From the front, many bikes have a single headlight with two amber running lights. The wattage of your headlight, even on high beam, may be no more than adequate under the best conditions. Add rain, traffic, or confusion on the part of oncoming drivers ("Is that a car with one headlight out?") and your trusty high beam may not be enough.

From the rear, where you are in danger of being overtaken or rear-ended, chances are that your bike is even less visible. Many bikes have nothing more than a single taillight, four to six inches across, that doubles as a brake light. In addition, rear-facing turn signals often are not illuminated as running lights. While this sort of stock lighting may be sufficient for recreational riders, it borders on criminally negligent for a distance rider planning to continue after dark and in all sorts of weather conditions.

Examine your options. Consider adding high-intensity lighting up front, like many of the riders in the Iron Butt do. At minimum, determine whether PIAA[6] makes a higher wattage bulb. You may

---

[5] See *www.performancebike.com/shop/Profile.html?SKU=5669&Store=Bike* for the Sigma Sport Diode Taillight.
See *www.roadrunnersports.com* for the RRS Reflective Clip.

[6] See *www.piaa.com* or discuss swapping bulbs with the local dealer for your bike's brand.

even want to consider high intensity discharge lighting, which uses no filament, but fires an electric charge between two electrodes in a xenon gas-filled bulb.[7] This is unquestionably the next upgrade for Eli, before another long trip.

Options for the rear of your bike require more creativity. One option is to wire your rear turn signals so they also function as running lights. Kits to accomplish this are available for many bikes. You should also determine whether dealers and aftermarket accessory manufacturers for your bike offer accessory taillights—either to mount on your saddlebags or to replace your stock taillight with something more attention getting. You may have seen traffic signals or truck taillights composed of dozens of extremely bright light-emitting diodes (LEDs). LED taillights are available for everyone from bicyclists to Corvette owners.[8] Do a web search for "LED taillights" or check with your local dealer.

Some riders also like aftermarket light flashers, which are supposed to attract additional attention by flashing when you touch the brakes—rather than simply showing a bright, steady brake light. Sources for flashers can be found in the classified advertisements or smaller display ads in most motorcycle magazines.

None of these modifications replace your good sense regarding dangerous conditions (fatigue, heavy rain, unusually difficult nighttime conditions). But if you employ a combination of these suggestions, chances are good you'll be significantly more visible under the worst circumstances.

---

[7] See *www.rmhid.com* for road lighting, or *www.bajadesigns.com* for off-road units.
[8] See, for example, one rider's clever solution at *www.xs4all.nl/-hkuijer/taillight.htm*.

RIDE

Riding Techniques: Ten Ways to Stay Safe

Having just completed a coast-to-coast ride, what did I gain from the experience? Here are 10 techniques that helped me make the trip safe and enjoyable.

1. Relax.

This sounds simple, but it's hard to do. Still, you'll arrive happier and ride better—if you learn to relax. The bike won't perform better just because you have a death-grip on the handlebars. Your motorcycle *knows* you are tense, but it lacks any ability to give back rubs or reassure you all will be well. So, relax! See Chapter 4 for more.

2. Be confident.

It's interesting, isn't it, that the first couple of riding techniques—perhaps two of the most important—are mental? While prudence is also required to complete a long trip successfully on a motorcycle, confidence is even more important. Never begin or continue a trip about which you cannot later say, "The successful outcome of the trip was never in doubt." Ride within your limits. Ride so you are always confident you can meet the changing conditions. When in doubt, slow down or stop. With confidence, you ride more relaxed. Without it, without knowing you are within your skill limits, you have crossed the line that represents the boundary of safety.

3. Turns are "push-push."

This is a corollary to *relax*. The best turns are made with a push in the direction you want the bike to go. Arm-wrestling the bars and fork, as a result of too much muscular tension, actually makes control more difficult. Also see technique four.

4. Believe in counter-steering.

Counter-steering is the reason push-push works. At road speeds, motorcycles turn *away* from the direction you point the front wheel. This approach is counterintuitive until you actually see it happen. Find a big deserted parking lot or road and try it on your own. Look at films of motorcycle racers and watch their corner entries in slow motion. If none of this helps, schedule a class with one of the good bike-handling schools like Keith Code's California Superbike School or Danny Walker's American Supercamp.[9]

5. Move your back end.

If you watch motorcycle racers, you immediately see that their bodies are almost always in motion, shifting from side to side on the seat. While you needn't go to that extreme, you extend the number of miles you can ride comfortably by moving around—instead of planting yourself in one spot from fuel stop to fuel stop. You'll also find that moving around allows you to handle the bike more confidently in certain situations (see technique six).

6. Your ability to turn is controlled only by throttle and lean angle.

In general, the more steeply you lean the bike, the quicker you turn. Lean angle is your primary turning tool. Use the throttle only to modify the results you get from a particular lean angle. If you need to move the bike one or two feet, more throttle swings you wider (not something you normally want) and less throttle tightens your turn. You'll get so you can put the bike on the exact line you want with slight adjustments to the throttle, while maintaining a constant lean angle. Remember "push it down."

---

[9] See *www.superbikeschool.com* and *www.americansupercamp.com*.

7. When all else fails, push the bike down farther.

Danny Walker's American Supercamp is invaluable for teaching the cornering techniques you need to get out of a tight spot. Shift your weight forward to get over the bike's center of gravity. Move up on top of the seat to remain perpendicular to the ground. An emergency is not the time to play pro and try to put a knee-puck on the ground. Good throttle control is also essential—particularly on slippery surfaces. But the key to using all these techniques it to "push the bike down." It's more difficult to describe, than to learn. Basically, it amounts to increasing the lean angle beyond the point you thought was comfortable. Before trying this on your own, consider investing in a two-day American Supercamp, to practice with Danny's Honda XR100s on a dirt track.

8. Find a gap.

This is your separation bubble. Increase speed or slow down to keep yourself within a gap in traffic where others aren't. You want space in front (at least two to three seconds) and, ideally, that much space behind. Your bubble should protect you to each side, also. Imagine an air traffic controller separating you from the traffic ahead, behind, and beside. Thankfully, as motorcyclists, we don't have to worry about traffic above and below! See Chapter 7 for a longer discussion of this technique.

9. Never, never, never accelerate quickly after a traffic light changes.

You'll be flattened, flattened, flattened. At the bottom of one freeway ramp, I avoided being hit by a speeding car, by hesitating almost *two full seconds* after the light changed. Look both ways. If you can, let "blockers" run interference for you, by keeping a car or truck in front of you. Keep one beside you, if it's a multilane road. This is *one* time that traffic alongside can be a safety factor, rather than a threat.

10. Finally, ride as if everyone around you is an idiot.

They're not, of course. Most drivers are very nice, intelligent people, who are just trying to go somewhere to do something else. But their minds are often on the "something else." More important, non-riders don't have a clue what your riding environment is like. They don't realize you lack the luxury of automatic stability, like their four-wheeled vehicles. They don't know you can't stop or turn instantly in the rain (they can't either, but most of them don't drive like they know that). They don't have your finely tuned senses that maintain balance, compensate for winds, watch for uneven paving between lanes…. The list is endless. The point is *you must ride defensively.* Assume motorists are unaware of your presence and your limitations, and you are a lot more likely to end every day of your trip safely.

Thoughts from the Road: Rows and Columns

POST I stopped the engine and parked well away from the mini-mart. I had threaded Eli between almost endless suburban office buildings to find a gas station and something to eat. Really, I just wanted a few minutes peace and quiet. The eastbound trip would end tonight, all being as planned, and I was looking forward to seeing family. But I wanted a few minutes to reflect on the miles covered.

Leaning against Eli, making notes in my journal, I spotted a car in my peripheral vision. It was headed diagonally across the gas station, directly for my bike. I looked up and through the car's windshield I could see the driver wearing a huge grin, with his thumbs in the air in a double thumbs-up sign. His mission accomplished, he turned to avoid the bike and disappeared back into traffic.

Maybe he worked in one of the nearby buildings. Rows and columns. Multiple floors stacked in rows, one atop the other. Multiple offices on each floor, making columns from top to bottom of the building. And offices filled with spreadsheets of rows and columns, columns and rows that will decide who works in the building next week—and who doesn't.

"How many years did you work for us…? Oh, we're very sorry. But with the recession, well, you know how it is…."

Who was the man with the grin? Only 13 days to Christmas. Would my smiling friend be victor or victim at year's end? A lot of people were given unexpected news for Christmas. Downsized. Collateral damage in a merger. Laid off. On the other hand, is it really a victory to remain while facing the same amount of work, with the same revenue and earnings pressures, aboard the same rudderless ship—with fewer people to make it all happen?

Lives affected. Families imperiled. Futures changed. All based on rows and columns; little cells; little boxes. But we're people. Our job is to stay out of boxes. Maybe the man with the grin saw my bike and understood that. Who knows? Perhaps an hour before, he had learned he no longer fit in the rows and columns at his company—but seeing Eli, he knew exactly what he'd do next.

Just ride. Go ride. Riding won't solve your problems, but it clears your head. And it opens your heart to the people and possibilities around you. I almost expect to see the grinning man wearing leathers and on a bike of his own, next time I'm between Biloxi and Greenville. I hope we both remember today. It'll be fun to hear him say, "Do you know how many years I worked for that company? But, well, you know…getting out of there was the best thing I ever did. Anyway—enough of that. Where you headed today, partner?"

Where am I headed? I'm gonna ride. Just ride.

Chapter 9:

The Long and Winding Road
Wednesday-Thursday, December 19-20
Greenville, SC to Luling, TX—1,099 Miles

The Trip:
A SaddleSore Day

TRIP

Eli had arrived in South Carolina happy and healthy, but due for service. At each 10,000-mile service increment, a good bit of inspection is done. Despite having the bike looked over and the oil changed in Tucson, I wanted all service current before heading back to California. I also wanted one last chance to make certain there were no lasting effects from the sand storm we hit between Indio and Blythe. So, during the week in South Carolina, Eli and I headed for Harley-Davidson of Greenville, to visit Wyatt Wilson's good shop.

H-D of Greenville had serviced Eli after the August trip. Their courtesy in getting Eli in and out quickly—not to mention a good bath and polishing, as well—was much appreciated. As a result, Eli was looking forward to this visit. And he emerged the next day in great shape and ready for the westbound crossing. It didn't take much imagination to hear his eagerness to be on the road again, seeing him relaxing in the winter sunshine and knowing that this temporary inactivity wouldn't last.

But as the departure date neared, I wavered. It would be so easy to ship the bike home again and catch a commercial flight, as I had in August. The total expense would be about the same—maybe *less* than riding. My family was also concerned about the amount of time I'd be spending on the road. And the lure of more time with my children during the Christmas season was strong. But in my moment of greatest weakness, Susan provided the kind of clear thinking that makes me grateful she is my wife.

"Look," she said. "You've been disappointed almost every day about not completing your roundtrip last August. Just get on the bike and ride!"

How could I refuse?

The evening before departure, my daughter and her husband gave Eli an early Christmas gift. They knew of my battles with seats wet from overnight dew, as well as sand and dirt from desert overnights. Their gift was a fitted Harley-Davidson motorcycle cover. How could I refuse? No more nights for Eli in the dampness and the cold. No more wrestling with tarps and bungee cords or improvising with plastic bags for me.

It would be nice to say that while preparing to ride home, I had also systematically prepared to qualify for an Iron Butt Association (IBA) award. But I hadn't. Months earlier, I had read a magazine account about a rider who attempted a 1,000-mile day—a "SaddleSore 1,000" as the IBA calls such a ride. Riders may boast over a beer, "Yeah, I did 1,000 yesterday," but mileage claims often prove to be inflated. The IBA—in addition to running the Iron Butt Rally during which riders travel 10-15,000 miles in 10 or 11 days—also certifies individual distance rides of 1,000 or more miles in a specified period of time. The IBA charges no membership fee, but you cannot join without riding at least 1,000 miles in less than 24 hours and having your ride certified.

SaddleSore 1,000 pin

The award is the coveted IBA license plate backing frame that says, "Iron Butt Association: World's Toughest Riders," along with a pin you can buy for your jacket or vest.

While a single 1,000-mile day doesn't approach the Herculean standard of the full Iron Butt Rally, I was encouraged to know that most rally participants begin by doing single-day qualifying rides before graduating to the Rally itself. Hoping to join that group, I wanted to devote at least one day during my trip to a SaddleSore 1,000. As I stood beside the gas pump, however, on this sunny morning in South Carolina, I reminded myself that *today might not be the day.* No get-there-itis. Just see how the day goes. Just ride. Take the 1,000 miles one step at a time.

The IBA's certification process for a SaddleSore 1,000 is rigorous. You must obtain signed statements from a witness at the start and finish of your ride, as well as dated, time-stamped receipts for each stop along the way. Before leaving Greenville, I stopped to say good-by to my daughter-in-law Amy and granddaughter Sophia. My departure from their house would become my official start time and Amy my cheerful sendoff witness.

Three hours later, I'd breezed through Atlanta. Compared with my last visit to Atlanta—after dark, in the rain, during rush hour—it was a pleasure to fly along their high occupancy vehicle (HOV) lanes in daylight and no rain. More and more cities have come to recognize that motorcycles are road- and environment-friendly. Our bikes require less space to park when commuting; the low weight of bike and rider has virtually no impact on road surfaces; our smaller engines burn less fuel and generate fewer emissions. Small wonder, then, that most cities offer motorcycle riders the chance to use HOV or carpool lanes to reduce traffic congestion and air pollution. Some cities (my hometown included) even give bikers free parking at preferred locations in city garages.

Unlike days when I had no definite goal, today's ride took on a more deliberate pace once past Atlanta. Gas stops were crisp, without being rushed. I consumed food and water with endurance objectives in mind. I spent less time talking with people during these breaks, though I had pleasant conversations at longer meal and rest stops.

The hours continued. Miles slid by. Near Satsuma, Alabama, I stopped for an early dinner. By then it was clear I could make it substantially farther than Biloxi, eclipsing the final day of the eastbound trip. What remained uncertain was how *much* farther.

"One step at a time," I reminded myself. "If Biloxi looks easily possible, then tentatively commit to Baton Rouge. Let's see how everything feels then."

By the time the exit signs pointed to Biloxi, I was proceeding westbound rapidly. Total elapsed time since leaving Greenville had been only a little more than eight hours, compared with the 12-hour day eastbound from Biloxi to Greenville—much of it in the rain. Winter's early darkness was beginning to surround us, but Eli purred along happily and in a couple of hours the outskirts of Baton Rouge came into sight. I pulled into a rest stop.

From there I made my first call home for computer support to confirm the distance needed. I had no idea Susan was suffering from the worst sore throat and flu she'd had in years.

"Heh-hello?"

"Hi, hon. I'm in Baton Rouge. Can you take a look on the Web and let me know exactly where 1,000 miles would be, to see if I can complete an Iron Butt ride tonight?"

Nothing in her voice suggested that this was the most unreasonable request she'd heard all day. Exhausted and feeling rotten, she nevertheless agreed to check while I was on the phone. A moment passed. She checked MapQuest and said that it looked like somewhere past Sealy, TX—another 320 miles—but before San Antonio would do it.

"Great! I'm going to try. I'll call you from farther down the road and double-check my mileage. Talk to you then."

In retrospect, it's best I didn't know how bad she felt. Knowing she was fighting the flu all alone would have sapped much of my energy. Obviously, I could have, and probably should have, simply checked a map. But because we had always worked together this way, getting support from home seemed natural during my brief stop in Baton Rouge.

More miles passed. I quickly tired of the uneven road surface in western Louisiana and eastern Texas. It bothered me more westbound than it had eastbound. And, it was clear by this time that serious effort would still be required to finish 1,000 miles in 24 hours. "Should-haves, could-haves" began to haunt my thoughts.

"I could have left Greenville earlier."

"I should have done more planning, to know exactly where the 1,000 miles would be complete. This is no way to ride a SaddleSore 1,000!"

But being within striking distance, I wasn't going to give up that easily.

Night wore on. Beaumont passed behind us. Darkness telescoped the distance between Beaumont and Houston. It was after 2 a.m. now. One huge advantage of passing through Houston this late was no traffic forced me to detour around the city on the

Sam Houston Freeway. That thought buoyed me for a while. Four lanes became six, and six became eight. I relished the thought of breezing through downtown Houston on an empty freeway.

I glanced to my left as the empty city spun by. I hadn't been in Houston for years, not since the 1970s for a convention held at the old Astrodome. The city was bigger than I remembered; certainly, it was better looking. Somewhere along the way I saw a billboard for the city's orchestra. I wondered how they compared to the Philadelphia Orchestra, which we loved so much when Susan and I lived there?

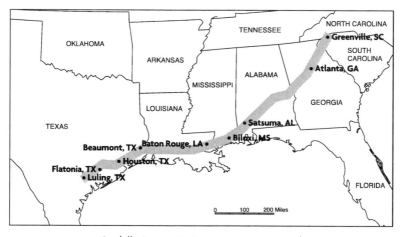

SaddleSore 1,000 territory covered

But before I had much more time to appreciate the empty city or reflect on the quality of the arts in Houston, it happened. It *was* happening. I was certain it happened *this* time. Earlier Eli's engine had seemed to miss a beat or stumble for a second or two. That was 10 miles ago. But if he did stumble, he recovered quickly and the big twin's comforting heartbeat continued through the night. This time, however, there was no mistaking it—the stumble, the belch. Something was wrong. But what? And what next? How could I end my attempt at a 1,000-mile day so close to my goal? Please, not now!

What to do? I don't need gas, but maybe the gas from the last fill-up was contaminated. C'mon, man—look! Think! Where will I find gas downtown at this time of night? Before resolving that issue, a more daunting thought came to mind. What if the bike stops entirely? What if this is the Immobilizer alarm problem? I know how to fix it. Before I left Santa Rosa, Jake had shown me how to swap plugs in the wiring harness under the seat. But it wouldn't be quick. Could I do it in the dark, beside a freeway in downtown Houston? And is Houston's downtown safe, unsafe, or something in between, at this time of night? The prospect of finding out—alone and on foot at 2 a.m.—was not a happy thought.

Nearing the western edge of downtown, I spotted what appeared to be a 24-hour mini-mart and filling station. Heart in my throat and a prayer on my lips, I signaled and moved toward the exit. The bike continued to stumble, almost as if water had been mixed with the fuel. I coasted down the exit ramp and blipped the throttle to keep the RPMs up. Forced to stop at the bottom of the ramp, I was especially careful not to kill the engine as we turned left and headed for the station. Slipping the clutch carefully and keeping the engine turning over at a much higher speed than normal, we made the station.

The doors of the mini-mart appeared locked and there were bars on the windows. The "should-haves, could-haves" came back in force. With just a little better planning, I could have avoided putting myself in this situation. No one was outside, although I could make out the movement of at least one person inside—a night clerk, perhaps? A clean-up person?

The gas pumps were card activated. With a gulp, I thumbed the kill switch and shut off the motor. Would it start again? Would I find out why there were bars on the windows? Quickly, I slid my card through the card reader. It seemed to take far longer than normal, but authorization was granted and gas started to flow.

The tank filled quickly. Eli hadn't needed much. I hoped that mixing fresh fuel might dilute whatever contaminants had found their way into the tank. Or maybe the force of fuel from the nozzle would dislodge something blocking the tank's fuel supply valve. Either way, would the engine start and run?

Put the pump on the hook. The pump didn't print a receipt. I'd have to note an exception for my SaddleSore documentation. Had everything in Texas stopped working at the same time? Tighten the gas caps. Look around quickly, to be certain nothing had dropped. Double-check. Is the bike in neutral? Deep breath... kill switch on again. Touch the starter. Hooray! Dear God be thanked. In the middle of the night, in an unfamiliar place, with my 1,000-mile goal in sight, the motor fired quickly. The pulsing high speed idle confirmed that the enricher knob was pulled out fully.

But, wait! Pulled out? How? I hadn't touched the enricher. The engine was hot. It didn't need a gas-rich mixture to start. Had I run all the way since my last gas stop with the enricher on? Could that have caused plug fouling that led to Eli's erratic performance over the last few miles? Had fatigue set in, so I didn't notice the enricher was pulled out? On the other hand, I'd occasionally left the enricher out longer than necessary, only to find that the knob seemed to return itself to a normal position.

Whatever the case, right now, just go! This was not the time for a complete diagnosis. I quickly dropped my left hand to the enricher knob, shoved it in, grabbed a handful of clutch and dropped the bike into gear. In an instant, Eli and I were gone. Keeping the RPMs up, I passed under the freeway and headed for the entrance ramp.

"Not smooth, not normal, but better," I thought, trying to sense what the engine was saying.

Copy of SaddleSore 1,000 log, submitted to IBA

"If I can just get through the light at the bottom of the entrance ramp and back on the freeway, I'll have a chance to open the throttle wide enough to blow out whatever might be fouling the plugs."

Rolling on power aggressively, Eli roared and responded with the rush that I expected from full throttle.

"Yes!"

Whatever the problem had been, it wasn't evident at full acceleration. The motor sounded and felt fine. I kept the engine speed up by remaining in fourth gear for a while, just to be sure anything that higher revs might cure was burned off or blown out before shifting. Best of all, the goal was still possible! One thousand miles might still be reached.

Sealy passed, and I stopped for gas at Flatonia, about 60 miles west of Sealy. Eli didn't need much fuel, but I didn't want to pass any opportunity, not knowing how many more stations down the road would be open all night. Equally important, I didn't want to finish the ride unable to get a dated and time-stamped receipt. Not knowing yet where I would stay, I wanted at least one valid receipt to confirm the distance—in the event no witness was available at the end of the ride.

The station was busy for 5 a.m. It still felt like the middle of the night for me, but was probably the beginning of the next day for most customers. It was cold. I snatched the receipt from the pump and dashed inside the mini-mart. Purchased a cup of coffee and a pastry, hoping my goal was close enough that this would be my last "meal" of the day. I wandered around inside long enough to warm up and phone Susan, who had spent the night tracking my progress.

She checked MapQuest again and it appeared I had officially finished the ride. But from the beginning I promised myself that, wherever the 1,000-mile threshold might be, I'd ride at least 50 miles beyond it just to have sufficient margin for error. My fatigue and Susan's sore throat both were both beginning to show. All I wanted to do was go to bed. Ironically, all Susan wanted to do was to go to bed, too—but she had this maniac husband calling her from the middle of Texas, demanding, "How much farther? Where am I and when can I stop?" After some back-and-forth consultation, it seemed that Luling, about 35 miles more, would give me a 50–80 mile safety factor to buffer any differences in

MapQuest's distance calculations and whatever system the Iron Butt Association might use. To ride 1,000 miles but not have the ride certified due to some small miscalculation would be heartbreaking.

Back outside, a couple of fellows in a pickup remarked, "Great bike."

"Thanks."

Eli *had* proven himself a great bike today, running 1,000 miles with only brief stops and not a minute of trouble—save the inexplicable (and possibly rider-induced) stumbling around Houston.

Ready for the last leg to be over, I pulled on my electric gloves, plugged in the jacket liner, and continued west. Perhaps I could make it as far as San Antonio.

Hard miles now. Tired and cold, I was ready for bed. Part of me wanted to make it to San Antonio just to say I'd done it. A much larger part of me just wanted to lie down and go to sleep. I'd been on the bike for almost 20 hours at this point. I found myself starting to slow down, a sign of increasing fatigue.

Determined to have a receipt from every possible endpoint for the ride, I pulled off the freeway at the next exit to get gas and look for a motel. As I reached the bottom of the exit and looked to my right, a deer stepped out of the shadows and into the grass between the exit and the frontage road. My heart sank. One of my biggest worries had been deer at night and my fear just became a reality. I gave silent thanks for having avoided any encounter with a deer at road speeds. Now I *knew* I wanted to be off the road.

After getting gas and checking the odometer mileage, I started the bike and scanned the exit area. There were two motels nearby. Choosing the more comfortable-looking of the two, I navigated the bike slowly toward the entrance, imagining the delicious comfort of clean sheets and a bed!

No one in the lobby.

"No, not now," I thought. "Not when it's OK for the trip to be over. Please come to the door. Answer the night bell."

Nothing. Helmet on again. Ride to the other motel. Helmet off. No one in the lobby. Ring the night bell. No answer.

"No, this can't be happening. Please answer the door." Nothing.

We were a forlorn pair, Eli and I, as we peered into the darkness looking west along I-10. What to do? If I wanted to sleep indoors—and I did—there was nothing to do but push on. Just ride. Who knows? Perhaps I'd make San Antonio, after all. That thought evaporated within five minutes of getting back on the freeway, when it became abundantly clear I needed rest.

The Luling exit appeared. I took it. There was nothing at the exit itself but a wooden sign promising the Coachway Inn a few miles north on Highway 90. Happy just to be off I-10, Eli and I cruised through the dark pre-dawn air, idling along, hopeful that Day One of the westbound trip was nearing its end.

The Coachway Inn came into view. For a moment, I feared the same result as at the previous two motels. But stepping into the brightly lit lobby, I was met by the night manager, who was efficient in providing a room—but equally important now—

A welcome site after 1,099 miles

Eli resting next to the Coachway Inn in Luling, TX

understanding about what I had just accomplished. He said he would be willing for the Iron Butt Association to contact him, if necessary, to attest to the end of my ride.

I parked Eli about an equal distance between the lobby and what turned out to be my first floor room—10 steps from the bike in either direction. Bags off. Fork lock on. Alarm set. Eli was comfortably nestled in an L-shaped nook between the lobby and my room. I was too tired even to try his new cover tonight. Hoping for his forgiveness, I took a hot shower and fell into bed, staying awake just long enough to call Susan, who was also happy to know I'd arrived safely. We could now both go off to sleep. The time in Texas was 6:17 a.m., CST, December 20, 2001—21 hours and 8 minutes since I first gassed up the bike in Greenville, SC.

Day One of the westward trip, and my SaddleSore 1,000, was finally over.

PREP

Pre-Trip Preparation: Plan Your Iron Butt Ride

When the ride became IBA certified, I learned I had traveled 1,099 miles from Greenville, SC, to the Coachway Inn in Luling, TX. As much as I would have liked seeing "San Antonio, TX" on my SaddleSore 1,000 certificate, I made the safe decision. Pushing on would not have been smart and would have been contrary to the IBA's intent that long distances are done *safely*.

But what might I have done better, before leaving home, to prepare for the SaddleSore portion of the ride? The top three things that would have made my 1,099-mile day easier are (1) plan, (2) plan, and (3) plan. Plan your route, plan your meals, and plan your endpoint. Even if you are a spontaneous, "Oh, let's try it today" type, you can improve your chances of success—and your certainty of safety—by planning.

Plan your route

I should not have been forced to phone Susan several times to know where the 1,000-mile endpoint was located. Think about it: a SaddleSore is easily doable, since most people are easily capable of remaining awake and functioning for 20 hours. Twenty hours at 50 miles per hour achieves the goal. And a 50 mph average allows for plenty of fuel, food, and rest stops, because you'll almost certainly be traveling faster than that over the road. If you decide to do an Iron Butt qualifying ride be sure to do the following.

Go to the Iron Butt site and review the rules. It would be disappointing to ride 1,000 miles—only to learn you came up a few miles short. It would be even more disappointing to ride the distance but fail to have your ride certified because you didn't follow the rules. Review the IBA site (*www.ironbutt.com*). Read the rules. Print out the forms you'll need.

Find a map and set your 1,050-mile course.   The extra 50 miles are margin for error. If you are completely confident you have a certifiable 1,000-mile course, you could get by with adding just 10 miles as a "comfort" factor. But don't ride something close to 15–20 hours and then fail to reach your goal because your map's distance-between-cities chart was wrong, or your guess based on "1 inch equals" was off.

Mark 150-mile legs on the map.   Your per-leg distance may vary if you have more endurance than I did, or your bike has a larger gas tank. But 150-mile increments give you six stops, seven legs. If you're in the western U.S., local speed limits allow you to complete 150 miles in a little more than two hours. Road conditions and speed limits in the eastern U.S. may make those three-hour legs. Either way, you still have adequate time (7 x 3 = 21 hours) for gas, food, and rest stops.

Plan your meals and rest stops

A 20-hour day of riding requires a lot of fuel—not only for your bike, but also for you. Make sure you get the proper food and liquids to maintain your energy and prevent dehydration. Keep your energy level up and you'll keep your average speed and attention-level up. Rest is also essential during a long-distance day. You're not going to get a two- or three-hour nap, but even a few minutes of rest are surprisingly refreshing. Note the following as you plan your food and rest stops for the day.

Eat an adequate breakfast, and know where you will eat lunch and dinner.   This assumes you'll be riding from early morning until after midnight. Have a good breakfast. Building your foundation for the rest of the day is important. Even if you don't normally eat a big breakfast, consider an omelet, potatoes, orange juice, and a good cup of coffee. "Breaking the back" of the 1,000 miles early—by riding strongly from Mile One, rather than gradually coming up to speed—is important. Then, try not to go more than four to five hours without a meal.

Establish a routine for meals and snacks during the day and maintain it.   We all have different metabolisms. Some people need to eat more less often while some people must eat less more often. The important thing is to understand your food needs and set a schedule.

For example, you may consider one of the following two approaches:

Every two legs, stop for a meal
   Doing so gives you four meals, counting breakfast. The meals after breakfast don't need to be big meals—in fact, you'll be less likely to be drowsy if they aren't. But every two legs, stop, get off the bike, take off your riding gear, and eat. You'll feel much fresher, if you do.

Or, every three legs, stop for a meal but snack at every stop
   Some people are not terribly sensitive to low blood sugar and hunger. However, I'm not one of them. When I get hungry, I get cranky and less efficient at whatever I am doing. Even so, I was able to complete this ride by stopping every three legs for a meal and having a good snack at each fuel stop. You know which foods work for you, but try to get something more than junk food. Choose stops that are likely to offer some choice. If you decide on this routine, when you do stop—even for snacks—hit the restroom and wash your face. The Iron Butt Association's "Archive of Wisdom" notes that just this simple act is refreshing and makes a significant difference in your alertness during your next leg.[1]

---

[1] Go to *www.ironbutt.com*, and click the "Archive of Wisdom" and read Tip #16.

Don't hesitate to stop more frequently if you need to. The SaddleSore 1,000, should be easily achievable with good planning and safe riding. If you need to stop for more frequent breaks—particularly as you near the end of the ride—don't hesitate to pull over for coffee or a stretch break that renews your ability to ride safely.

Plan your endpoint

Call ahead to reserve a room where you plan to stop. This is the one exception to my general rule that riders stay flexible about stopping for the night. I made a mistake not knowing the endpoint for my SaddleSore. As a result, I had to ride farther than necessary and ended up in a hotel that was less comfortable than I would have preferred. While the folks were very pleasant, it would have been nice to wake up in a place with a restaurant that served breakfast. Instead, I had to get on the bike and ride some distance before eating.

By calling ahead for your endpoint reservation, you also ensure you have a willing witness for the end of your ride. Ask to speak with the manager and be certain that she or he will sign your witness form and respond to the IBA, if asked. At least have him or her alert the front desk staff who will be on duty when you arrive, to head off any surprise or concern that you are asking them to do something contrary to policy. Sounds funny, but it happens. I was thankful that the night manager at the Coachway Inn was accommodating. Not everyone has the mindset of a rider crossing America by motorcycle. You don't want to run into someone at the end of your SaddleSore who responds, "Oh, I don't know if I can do that or not!"

EQUIP

Your Equipment: What Do I Wish I'd Had?

What equipment will be most important, if you do a SaddleSore 1,000? We each have our own answers to that question, but there are two items on my list.

The piece of equipment I most regret *not* having is an electronic deer whistle (see Chapter 6, "Your Equipment" section). While I'm still not convinced they prevent collisions, every possible precaution is warranted. I would equip my bike with the most powerful possible electronic whistle from Hornet.[2]

The second piece of equipment I regret not having is high intensity lighting (see Chapter 8, "Your Equipment" section). High intensity lighting would have made me feel safer, both in terms of visibility—the ability of motorists to see me—and early-warning— my ability to see a deer, or an obstacle, earlier.

Adding these two items presupposes you have the basics in place: a reliable bike, a comfortable seat, and a large enough fuel tank to ride 1,050 miles with six or fewer stops. Certainly, you can complete the ride successfully if you must make more stops. But you will have a larger buffer for fuel stops, meals, and unanticipated delays if you can ride 150 to 200 mile stretches without stopping.

RIDE

Riding Techniques: A SaddleSore is 90% Mental

The most important riding technique you'll need to employ for a SaddleSore 1,000 is not physical. It is mental. It's exercising good judgment.

---

[2] See *www.deer-whistle.com*, and consider the 135 dB S-135 model for interstate use. See their frequently asked questions (FAQs) at *www.xp3hornet.com/faq.shtml#28difference*

Pre-think as many dimensions of your trip as possible. The more you do in advance to promote safe riding, the better your trip will be. This is why it's best to do your advance planning well.

En route, apply all the standard rules for scanning, maintaining good situational awareness, and riding within your limits. In this respect, not much differs from normal riding. The big risk is that you focus so intently on your goal—on riding the distance—that you neglect the things that keep all motorcyclists safe.

Finally, recognize that your attention may wander especially near the end of your 1,000-mile day. Be vigilant to the warning signs of loss of attention or lack of control. As the Iron Butt Archive says, if you close your eyes *even for a moment* while on the road, pull over and rest. Distance motorcycle riding is a great pleasure and provides a wonderful sense of accomplishment. The SaddleSore 1,000 is akin to a motorcyclist's marathon. But no one runs a marathon consciously risking death. Runners are warned about the symptoms of heatstroke, of dehydration, of physical exhaustion. Aid stations are positioned throughout the course. Paramedics and EMTs are typically on hand to deal with any emergency.

On a SaddleSore 1,000 or BunBurner 1,500 (riding 1,500 miles in 36 hours), you become your own coach, aid provider, and paramedic/EMT. Exercise the kind of judgment that allows you to complete the ride safely and within your limits. Doing so enhances the feeling of accomplishment. You alone, through your planning and physical endurance, governed yourself and the ride in such a way that successful completion was never in doubt.

And now, even before you've finished the ride, let me be the first to congratulate you on a job well done. Special congratulations on the *mental* job of making your hours in the saddle as safe and enjoyable as possible.

Staying Organized: Remembering Your Trip

Making a long distance trip almost demands keeping a journal of some sort. Your notes capture the things photographs can't—thoughts that come to you as you ride; the names of places you'd like to revisit; improvements you'll want to make to your bike based on the experience gained during your trip; even new priorities about what's most important when you get home, which you now see with greater clarity.

Before you depart, think what will work best for you. You may want to carry a miniature tape recorder and dictate notes at each stop. You may be content with a simple notepad, as I was. Or you may go so far as to carry a palmtop or laptop computer to record mileage, costs, and your impressions as you ride. You may also want to carry a camera, a topic covered in Chapter 11.

Whatever your preferred way of for keeping a journal, the best equipment you can have for writing while riding is a good memory. Take the opportunity to work on your short-term memory, using techniques easily learned. First, associate whatever you want to remember with a picture—something visual. For example, if you want to remember to visit the Texas hills around Kerrville again, because it was so warm and sunny midwinter, then picture a bright golden sun with a big "K" emblazoned on it.

When pictures don't work, try alliterating everything you need to recall, making a mental list in which every item starts with the same letter. For example,

"Fifteen, foot, frantic"

might help bring back these recollections:

- It was *fifteen* miles outside Mobile, AL, where you saw the restaurant you want to try on the way home .

- Your *foot* pegs haven't been as comfortable as you'd like for a long trip, so look for options at your next stop.
- The traffic through Atlanta was absolutely *frantic* at rush hour, so find a way to bypass or avoid rush hour on the return trip.

Finally, try arranging thoughts in a specific, visual order in your mind. I found that if I had several things to recall, I could create mental images of them "lined up" in two rows—one above the other. Picture #1 would be top left. Picture #2 would be below it and just to its right. Picture #3 would be farther right but back on the top row, and so on. By the end of the trip, I could remember as many as a dozen main points, with three to five sub-points below the main points. Recalling things visually, you can also recite them to yourself forwards or backwards. This is more fun than memorizing Shakespeare, which cannot be said backward (at least not easily).

Whatever system works for you, you'll find yourself increasingly thankful for rest stops, which provide an opportunity to jot down the stack of items you've accumulated in your short-term memory, as well as the other kinds of relief a rest stop provides!

 ## Thoughts from the Road: On Distance Riding

POST

If your SaddleSore or BunBurner ride is anything like mine, you won't think about much else that day. Early in the day, your thoughts will be occupied with logistics and the challenge of doing 1,000+ miles. At the end of the day, your only thoughts will be about finishing safely and getting to sleep. Between those two extremes, you'll focus on collecting receipts and getting proper nutrition.

But 1,000 miles is a long way. You'll certainly need to be attentive to the traffic and situations around you. Threats never wait for attention. Be prepared to address them immediately, to anticipate them, just as you would if you were only riding a busy two or three miles from your home to a nearby destination.

Similarly, you'll employ the same strategies for fighting boredom (if you tend to get bored riding long distances). See Chapter 6 for a review of such strategies.

But the most important thoughts during your SaddleSore will be those that help you maintain the confidence that *you can do it*. If you have planned well, 1,000 miles may be an easy ride. And after you have completed a 1,000-mile ride, you may decide to try a 1,500 mile BunBurner. And if you have completed a BunBurner, you may be ready for multiple days of distance riding—maybe even the Iron Butt Rally itself.

At some point, however—whether on your distance ride or at some later time—you will need to coach yourself to finish the job, with a strong, positive attitude. When my son, Bob, ran the Chicago Marathon in 2001, I visited the marathon web site[3] to prepare for our trip to support his run. The motto for the race that year was "Strength over time, mind over matter, victory over doubt." To complete 1,000 miles or more in 24 hours, you need all three attributes. Begin thinking about strength over time. Be prepared to spend the miles in the seat. Do your advance planning, pre-thinking. Having done so, you will have gone a long way toward ensuring mind over matter. The mental discipline will prevail over the hours and unanticipated obstacles of the trip.

Perhaps the biggest challenge any marathoner or any distance rider faces, however, is to achieve victory over doubt. It is so easy to say, "I can't do that" and never start. It is so tempting to say, "I'm not sure I can finish" and stop short of your goal. The challenge of

---

[3] See *www.chicagomarathon.com*.

achieving victory over doubt exists, even when you begin by simply getting on your bike and crossing America.

Do it. Just do it. Just ride. You *can* do it. You can *control* your ride and *complete* it safely. You can achieve victory over doubt by proceeding one step at a time. I have a friend, Dennis, who is a weight trainer. He and I talk from time to time about what it requires to achieve strength goals; what it takes to discipline ourselves to be faithful to the training programs we have set.

Dennis' answer? "Just show up."[4] Just put on your T-shirt and shorts and show up at the gym. On the hard days, don't even tell yourself you have to lift anything. Just show up. If you are a runner, don't even tell yourself you have to go farther than to the end of your driveway to pick up the newspaper. Just get on your shoes and show up outside your house. If you are a SaddleSore rider, don't even think about the end of the ride or the difficulties of putting in a 1,000-mile day. Just get back on the bike after each rest stop and say to yourself, "We'll go as far as we can go, safely."

Don't give doubt a chance. Just show up. You'll find—like I did—this mental approach works for whatever we want to achieve in life off the bike, too.

---

[4] Dennis Moss, Sebastopol, CA.

SaddleSore 1,000 official certificate from IBA

Iron Butt Association license plate frame

Chapter 10:

Does Anybody Really Know What Time it Is?

Friday, December 21
Luling, TX to Ozona, TX—262 Miles

TRIP

The Trip:
A Short Day

Although a significant part of the country remained to be crossed, doing a SaddleSore 1,000 on the first day jump-started the return. Now I can take some easy days and still be home for Christmas. By putting 1,099 miles, out of the 3,000 I need to do, behind me yesterday, I felt as if I was home already. Months ago, even weeks earlier, the whole trip had seemed impossible. Just do it. Just go. Just ride.

Morning came late in Luling. Getting to bed just shortly before 7:00 a.m., I set an alarm for 10:30—wanting to be sure I was out before checkout time. I'd take it easy the rest of the day and not make any huge push for additional mileage.

Time to go. Packed the bike and checked out just before 11:00. Even after 1,099 miles yesterday, it was good to touch Eli again this morning. Why do we think our bikes are beautiful? We do; they are. He was a pleasure to behold. He was healthy, too, despite his night in the open air.

He started and ran well. Bright morning sun shone around the bike and warmed my back. Have you ever noticed that sunshine cures almost everything? The sun was a welcome contrast to the 28-degree temperature when I checked in last night. But the sun also seemed to warm my attitude and brighten the prospects of pressing on, after only three and a-half hours sleep. That much sleep would seem a luxury to Iron Butt Rally participants.

I had to be on the road, if only to make it across Texas today. Soon however, I began to doubt the likelihood of achieving even that. Texas is more than 850 miles across on I-10. Despite almost reaching San Antonio yesterday, 607 miles of the state remained. To make El Paso by nightfall would not be a short day.

Pulling out of the gas station, I headed west. Near Seguin, TX, I noticed an immense billboard for vasectomy reversals. Apparently this microsurgery had been perfected somewhere near Houston. In any event, it was now being offered to motorists along I-10. I wondered whether this offer was uniquely attractive to Texans, until I saw the same billboard along I-10 in California. Maybe the surgery is something especially desirable to travelers? You have to assume the folks offering this service researched and segmented their market, and understand why they are spending ad dollars for billboards on I-10.

Green grass reappeared today! After the long, dark hours spent crossing the Gulf states last night, the fresh grass in the sunshine was like a symbol of life; of rebirth. Probably the new grass had sprouted as a result of the hard rains that hit Texas only days after I passed through on my eastward journey.

I stopped in Kerrville, TX, west of San Antonio, for lunch. Kerrville had looked like a great place as I was heading east and I'd made a mental note to try to stop on the way home. My timing and the weather couldn't have worked out better.

An enjoyable lunch stop in Kerrville, TX

Among other things that distinguish the city, including the beautiful Texas hill country surrounding it, Kerrville has long been the home of Mooney Aircraft. Most pilots admire Mooneys for their speed and fuel efficiency. For a single engine airplane, it flies faster and on less fuel than others in its class. Sadly, the company has had repeated financial difficulties during its history. The present was no exception. But the company's rugged, responsive little airplanes had earned a place in my heart—the Porsche of aviation. I hoped that someone who appreciated them as much as I do would appear to spark the company's revival once more.

Without knowing exactly what I wanted to see, I exited for Kerrville, intent on making a loop that would ultimately put me back on I-10 at the next interchange. Along the way I spotted a restaurant offering outdoor seating and fish filets. I stopped and parked the bike behind the restaurant, near some picnic tables and a stream behind their property. Cypress trees of a different sort than we have in California lined the opposite bank. I wouldn't have been able to identify the trees at all, except for a friendly mountain biker sitting at the next table finishing his lunch. As it turned out, he had family in Petaluma, only a few miles from Santa Rosa, where my trip had begun. We enjoyed the lovely summerlike afternoon together and I lingered longer than planned. Still, stops like this are part of what crossing America is all about.

By the time I left Kerrville, it was clear today was going to be a short day. No dinner in El Paso tonight. The great lunch, warm sunlight, and throb of Eli's engine were all making me drowsy. Checking a map, it appeared that opportunities to stop would be few. Ft. Stockton, where I'd stayed on the trip east, was clearly beyond my reach. I resolved to exit at the next likely interchange and have a look at possible accommodations.

Ozona, TX, offered the Circle Bar Motel, restaurant, and store. I could stop now, fill up the bike, and get a good night's rest—or I could push on, and risk over-riding my abilities today. I shut off the engine and covered the bike. Day Two of the return trip was done.

Pre-Trip Preparation: After a Long Ride

PREP

After reading about my SaddleSore 1,000, you may be saying to yourself, "No way!" OK, don't ride 1,000 miles. But, I'd encourage you to at least consider starting your trip home with a long day. Getting some solid mileage under your belt early in the trip provides a huge mental boost that makes the rest of the trip seem easy. I didn't have that benefit on the eastbound trip, and the delays in getting out of California were discouraging. I don't necessarily want the trip to end, but I am glad for the long day yesterday because it brings the sense of accomplishment of journeying across America and back just a little closer.

Before attempting your long day(s), however, learn from my mistakes. Some of the consequences of my poor planning were not apparent until today. Having ridden only 261 more miles today after 1,099 yesterday, what are the lessons?

First, *start every long day early*. By not beginning my SaddleSore 1,000 until roughly 10 a.m., I had to ride through the night—resulting in today's late start. If you begin *your* SaddleSore early, you'll be able to stay on a more nearly normal schedule. That's healthier and safer. It also means you can get a normal start on the subsequent day, rather than departing midday, as I did. The late start reduced my average for two days to something only slightly greater than the distances I'd have achieved normally. I made progress today, but not much.

Second, *know your endpoint*. My SaddleSore 1,000 was probably complete at 4 a.m., but it was 6:17 a.m. before I checked into the motel. Even with my late start, I could have had two hours extra sleep if I had marked maps and picked an endpoint. Part of the extra two hours and 17 minutes was the result of wanting to be certain I'd completed 1,000 miles. Part of it was simply the result of not being able to find a motel. Hearing the alarm this morning, I regretted not planning my endpoint in advance. Even if you don't have your long ride certified, don't allow the freedom we riders enjoy enslave you unintentionally, forcing you to ride longer than you'd like because you didn't pick an endpoint and investigate lodging options.

Third, *fill up your bike before going to bed*. Fill your tank every night, even after a long day, so you don't have to delay starting the next morning. Finishing the job won't take long, and, as attractive as going to sleep immediately after your long day might seem, you'll thank yourself the next day for filling up your bike the night before.

Finally, *stay in a motel that offers breakfast*. In addition to fueling your bike, plan for the fuel you will need the next morning. Stay somewhere that offers a truly restorative breakfast, either at the motel or within walking distance. And make that a *good* breakfast, not just a quick mini-mart snack. You've earned the right to eat well this morning. Enjoy it, and splurge!

Your Equipment: Bike Covers

EQUIP

Let's talk about bike covers. I wanted one before leaving California, but there are limits to the amounts most of us can spend before a trip. As a result, I concentrated on good luggage and proper clothing for the expected weather. But I also spent a fair amount of time looking around motorcycle shops and searching eBay[1] for a motorcycle cover, for something I wanted and could afford. I was very pleased when my daughter and her husband presented their early Christmas gift—the perfect cover.

Here are the three most important features of a cover—The Three D's: design, durability, and disclosure.

Design

Unless you plan to wait for your bike to cool completely every time you cover it, buy a cover designed to be used the way you want to use it. The cover should be made in such a way—and from the proper materials—that pulling it over the bike does not endanger fabric next to the hot surfaces. On a local ride, I once dropped a lightweight bag designed to hold my goggles on Eli's muffler. Its fabric melted instantly. You don't want the same thing to happen to your cover. For that reason, you won't be satisfied with a nylon camping tarp or an inexpensive cover. Companies that specialize in making motorcycle covers, like DowCow (who makes Harley-Davidson's eagle-branded

---

[1] See *www.ebay.com,* and click the "Motorcycles" link in the Categories list on the left side of the page. Search for "motorcycle cover." You'll probably want to search just the ad titles, not titles and descriptions, for best results.

covers),[2] design their products to be used how you will actually use them. Think twice before substituting something less expensive. It's likely it will either self-destruct or prove unsatisfactory.

Eli snug in his bike cover

Durability

If you purchase a good cover, durability is almost assured. But if you are still considering an improvised solution employing tarps and bungee cords, remember the stresses your cover has to endure. The morning I woke up in Ozona, the wind was blowing so hard that Eli was trembling in the wind—like a small aircraft straining against its tie-down ropes, wanting to fly. But the cover was firmly in place, as expected. It's difficult to get the kind of durability and protection you'll want in all

---

[2] See *www.dowco-inc.com/mcycles.html*.

kinds of wind and weather, without buying a cover made specifically for your bike. Even then, the quality of covers varies widely. Expect to invest more than $100–150, depending on the make and model of your machine and the manufacturer of the cover. While your initial investment may seem high, years of satisfactory use make a good cover cheaper over time. You'll also have a greater chance of avoiding unpleasant surprises when you come out of your motel room each morning.

Disclosure

My initial reason for wanting a cover was to protect the seat and handlebars (the surfaces of the bike that a rider makes contact with) from moisture. During my August crossing of America, I endured several occasions—after parking for dinner or upon leaving in the morning—when Eli's seat was soaked. To prevent this unpleasantness, a cover seemed the best answer. But after using the Harley/DowCow cover during my westbound trip, I came to appreciate its ability to protect *the entire* bike from prying eyes and potential thieves. Some motorcyclists deliberately ride "rat bikes" for that reason. Nothing about a rat bike appears to be worth a thief's attention. But if your motorcycle is a brand or model attractive to thieves, or has chrome and exotic accessories, covering the bike all the way to the ground—including the tires—is cheap additional insurance. I felt more secure. Eli stayed clean and dry. I'll never leave a naked bike in a motel parking lot again.

Riding Techniques: Freeway Exits

RIDE

If you're crossing America for the first time, you may be amazed at the different types of freeway exits you will encounter. So, while discussing freeway exits might seem elementary, even unnecessary, the information in this section may save your bacon at exactly the time you need it most. If I had just paid a little more attention to exit configurations, I would have avoided a close call that required some fancy riding to save my trip.

Thankfully, the consequences of my misjudgment were not severe. No injury or damage to the bike resulted. But it could have. And the incident produced a much-increased heart rate for several minutes.

What happened was this: I left the freeway for a routine gas stop. As good riders should do, I mentally scanned the general characteristics of the exit. Downhill. Asphalt, rather than concrete. Dusty, but not seriously so (for example, there was no blowing sand). The exit was more than long enough to allow deceleration on the exit itself. Finally, at the end, I'd turn left and go back under I-10 to reach the gas station. Scan completed, I thumbed my right-hand signal and rolled off power as I headed down the exit.

Near the bottom of the exit, however, three additional characteristics became apparent. First, the exit did not simply descend, but hooked sharply to the right near the bottom. Second, there was a large concrete culvert left of the hook, which would seriously punish any rider who missed the hook.

But neither of these attributes would have been dangerous, except for a third. Contrary to my expectation, the exit didn't end in a "T" against the road passing under the interstate. The hook dumped exiting traffic onto a frontage road. Crossing traffic was expected to yield, but does a motorcyclist *ever* trust intersecting traffic to yield or stop? No.

Now the situation was dangerous:

- I'm headed down the exit ramp at moderate speed
- However, the exit unexpectedly terminates in an tight hook (heads-up)

- There is a pit to punish the unwary (this is becoming more serious)
- The road is dusty, reducing traction (sharp braking won't work)
- And traffic suddenly appears on the frontage road (now we have problems!)

I squeezed the front brake with increasing pressure, being careful not to lose traction. I applied increasing force to the rear brake, when—abruptly!—the rear wheel breaks loose and slides toward the concrete culvert. Can I remain upright, stay out of the pit, and avoid the intersecting traffic?

As much as I'd *like* to claim credit for skillfully avoiding the crash, I think this was one of those "there but for the grace of God" situations. Everything happened so fast, the danger was already past when one foot hit the pavement harder than intended and I realized my heart rate was stratospheric. But the bike was stopped and upright. So how much can be deduced about what happened?

As soon as the rear wheel broke loose, I corrected by turning the front wheel into the slide like a dirt-tracker. Once again, I was thankful for my training at Danny Walker's American Supercamp.[3] My reaction to the slide was automatic. In the same way you steer into a skid when driving a car on ice, steering into the slide on the ramp stopped my slide toward the pit and decelerated the bike to a point that stopped short of intersecting traffic. The sliding drills we did during my two Supercamps (particularly the mud drill, the wet track drill) had their intended effect. Other than a slightly sore foot from abruptly bracing the bike as it slid to a stop, no harm was done and my trip continued uneventfully.

---

[3] See *www.americansupercamp.com* or call 970 669-4322. Also see Chapter 8, technique number 7, under "Riding Techniques." This was not an example of pushing the bike farther down, but of one more of the many valuable skills you will learn and practice in Danny's camps.

Learning to slide on a dirt track

The point here, however, is not a primer on Texas exit ramps. The first point is to know how to handle your bike in any situation. The second is that exits vary widely from state to state—and even within states. It would be impossible to catalog every exit shape. For example, New Jersey state highways often use jug handles at major intersections. For these, you exit right—despite your desire to turn left. You won't find a left turn lane like you'd expect in most states. But New Jersey freeway ramps terminate normally, in a straight line against the intersecting road. Contrast that with Wisconsin and Texas (to name just two examples), where the exits often crisscross frontage roads, which makes it difficult to know where to go and who should yield.

Maybe you've ridden tens of thousands of miles without any difficulty at the bottom of an exit. Great. Here's to your health! May your success continue. But maybe, *just maybe*, there's an exit still lurking out there, waiting for you—one that will throw you an unexpected curve. Maybe it will be a decreasing radius turn, a slick spot on the pavement, an exit-ending you can't decipher at normal speeds, or intersecting traffic that should yield, but doesn't.

If that exit is still somewhere in your future, I'll feel justified including this section. And if that's the case, send me an email to let me know that being just a little more careful about exits saved your bacon, too.

Thoughts from the Road: The Ambivalence of Affluence

POST

The journey back to California has not felt like a new trip, but simply like resuming a conversation begun long ago. Like picking up where you left off with a long-time friend, the thoughts that returned during my riding hours had a familiarity that was comforting, calming.

Riding today, it was pleasant to think about what life might be like if we all made a pact to slow down. "When in doubt, slow down or stop." I had jotted down that thought earlier in my trip, about riding technique. But might it also be applied to our lives? I see people every day (I have been one of those people) who cram so much into each day, each week, opportunities to enjoy each moment are missed. This frenzy afflicts everyone from manager to minister, and doesn't discriminate on the basis of race or gender.

What a contrast for those of us who grew up singing along with Chicago:

Does anybody really know what time it is?
Does anybody really care?[4]

---

[4] "Does Anybody Really Know What Time It Is?" Written by Robert Lamm © 1969 (Renewed) Lamminations Music/Aurelius Music (ASCAP). Used By Permission. International Copyright Secured.

When did we lose that sense of the irrelevance of—in fact, the absolute harm of—haste?

The loss is not simply our own. In our frenzied activity, we lose the chance to do craftsman-like work for others. We turn out shoddy products and offer shoddy service. We lose track of the small and large threads of our lives—remedying household problems, writing notes to friends, mending clothes, remembering birthdays, caring for our gardens, keeping up with world events. When war erupted in Yugoslavia, few even knew where the country was located. Fewer of us have a basic understanding of the history behind today's conflict in the Middle East.[5] We say, "But, I have no time."

We even fail to slow down long enough to thank others, or to be thanked in ways that are truly thoughtful. You can't show gratitude to the chronically busy. They don't have time to be thanked. We lose the habit of thinking in a way that would allow us to *recognize* sacrifices made by others as an expression of thanks. Our thank yous and theirs become no more than ritual gestures, executed speedily and supported by impersonal industries conceived for this purpose.

A good friend in Colorado introduced me to the notion of the "ambivalence of affluence."[6] It might just as easily be called the "exhaustion of excess." His point was that most of us have so much, have so many choices, we actually become paralyzed by trying to decide what to do next. We become modern day equivalents to

---

[5] For nights during your next long ride, consider taking along *A Peace to End All Peace*, by David Fromkin (New York: Avon Books, 1989). And while, sadly, Yugoslavia is only a memory for much of the world today, Slavenka Drakulić's *How We Survived Communism and Even Laughed* (New York: Harper Collins, 1991), remains a highly readable first person perspective on a world falling apart.

[6] Dr. David Caster, see *www.oldtown-guesthouse.com*, 888 375-4210, Colorado Springs, CO.

Eliot's previously mentioned Prufrock, except our lament would sound something like this:

> *Shall I stay at home today? Is anything out of reach?*
> *No, I shall fly an aeroplane, or walk upon the beach.*
> *My Palm just chirped, more meetings planned,*
> *They stack up, each by each.*
> *Friendships lost; moments gone–*
> *I do not think that they will seek for me.*[7]

No, those moments, those friendships won't seek us. We must seek them. And that's what a ride like this is about. Start making your dreams real. Get on the bike. Stop to visit friends you haven't seen in a while. Just go. Ride—just ride.

---

[7] With apologies to T.S. Eliot, for the paraphrase of his poem, "The Love Song of J. Alfred Prufrock." I trust he would understand. See page 80 for the original version.

Chapter 11:

Waterfalls

Saturday, December 22
Ozona, TX to Las Cruces, NM—392 Miles

The Trip:
Another Distance Rider

Dawn came cold and windy. Eli seemed to quiver in the blasts, but was snug under his cover. Jerking my fleece hat low over my ears, I jogged crablike, with my back to the gusts, through the parking lot to the restaurant. If the weather didn't change soon, this promised to be a long day. Breakfast wasn't special, but it was warm. Bike cover off. Secure the luggage. Plug in the electric jacket liner and gloves. Let Eli idle a bit longer than normal—longer, at least, than normal for California's mild winters.

Home! I'd be home in California again in four, maybe three, days.

Wish I'd brought a swimsuit. The Circle Bar had a heated indoor pool. It would have felt good last night just to relax in the warm water. For that matter, it wouldn't feel bad right now.

With distance, the weather improved. By the time I reached Ft. Stockton, the sun shone brightly. It was time for lunch. Pulling into yet another mini-mart, I filled up the bike and parked by the store. Their food selection was nothing special, but they did stock a favorite bike aid: Armor All Wipes. These wipes are diaper technology made good! While polishing the dirty bottoms of my fiberglass saddlebags, I noticed a man and woman pulling in, trailering purple Honda Gold Wing.

"How ya doin'?" they asked.

"Pretty good, thanks. Just taking a break."

"Yeah. Know the feelin'. Just rode Myrtle Beach. Did 582 miles the last day."

I had no idea why they were trailering the bike right now, but if they put in a 600-mile day together on the purple Wing, they were riders. Good for them!

Later in the day, I met another distance rider, Paul, from Houston. He was headed to Oregon, on a well-equipped Yamaha tourer with fairings, a GPS, CD player, and a communications system (at least, he wore a helmet with a microphone, presumably for a citizen's band radio or for a passenger). I followed him for a while before we actually met. He rode straight and true, maintaining good lane position, despite the wind. When he saw me in his mirrors, he dropped back and waved. We fell into a rhythm that kept our bikes together for some miles.

Paul stopped for gas. Eli didn't need gas, but I followed him into the station and parked near the street, away from the pumps.

"Hey, just wanted to say hello," I began.

"Thanks. Good riding together. You headed far?"

We fell into the natural course of subjects that riders discuss—destinations, routes, winds and adverse conditions, and each other's bikes.

"You really crossed the U.S. on that?" he asked, pointing to Eli.

"Yep—1,000 miles on Monday."

"Aw, man. That's a long day. 750 is about my best day so far."

Nothing wrong with a 750-mile day. This man was a real rider. Paul's machine clearly showed that he used and appreciated it.

"I'm heading out," I said. "Ride safe."

Paul waved as I turned west from the station and rolled on power. He would do the miles between here and Oregon just fine.

Purchasing gasoline was a pleasure in Texas. Yesterday, I'd gotten 93-octane for as little as $1.08 per gallon! The highest octane we can get in California (off a racetrack) is 91-octane and it seldom sells for less than $1.50 per gallon—sometimes as much as $2.00. Later on in the trip, I realized I'd been lulled into gas-price complacency. Back in California, prices jumped dramatically.

Now I need gas again. Standing at the pumps, I was reminded that as the trip wore on to conclusion, I was becoming less tolerant of the rude intrusions modern marketing makes into our lives. Earplugs may prove most useful, not for minimizing wind and road noise, but for blocking recorded messages and music that plays at many mini-mart fuel pumps. One particularly offensive stop today included a taped advertisement that said (over, and over, and over):

> *Uh oh! Forgot to buy holiday dinner? Try our crispy chicken. It's . . . (blah, blah, blah) good . . . and it won't cost you a wing and a leg.*

Who makes up this nonsense? Aside from intruding upon silence (or at minimum, the ordinary sounds of daily life), this advertisement was insulting. Were all of us gassing up our vehicles supposed to be bent over in belly laughs at "a wing and a leg"? Worse still, think about what the underlying premise says about our lives—we pay so little attention to the events that mark our passing of years, we even forget to buy holiday dinner. Will we feel better about ourselves because a recorded voice and a bad joke suggest we buy some fried chicken?

I was glad to get out of the station and back on the road.

Texas appears to have a great enthusiasm for the color pink. As I passed near Seguin yesterday, three sights—all bright pink— presented themselves: a billboard for Chevy Silverado pickups, the Gage Furniture store (clearly visible from I-10), and the O'Fiesta Restaurant. In other parts of the country, bright pink would be associated with roadside adult bookstores or lingerie shops. I was curious about this local affinity for pink. But the farther I rode along I-10, the clearer it became that wind, not pink buildings, would occupy most of my attention today.

Approaching El Paso late in the afternoon, I could see what looked like haze hanging over the area. The wind continued unabated. As I got closer, it was clear—once again—I was entering a dust storm. I had hoped to stop at Barnett's Harley-Davidson, east of El Paso. Reportedly, they are the largest Harley dealer in the world, with 400–500 bikes in stock at any given time. However, by the time I exited I-10, blowing dust and sand completely obscured any distant view. I wandered around the area for five or ten minutes without finding the dealership and returned to the freeway.

Fighting rush hour traffic, sand, and dust along I-10, I didn't see a place sufficiently attractive to lure me off the bike for the night. Near the west edge of town, I finally spotted an exit with several choices for gasoline and food. It was growing dark. At a minimum, I needed gas. Food would have been nice, too, but wasn't essential yet.

As I pulled into the station, who appeared but Paul from Houston. Obviously he had done better in the West Texas wind than I had. He must have passed me while I was stopped for gas near Barnett's H-D. He'd already gassed up and was headed out. We waved. I pulled up to a pump and stopped the engine.

Without a decent hotel nearby, I pulled on my now-dusty helmet once more and rolled down the entrance ramp toward I-10. The next town of any size was Las Cruces, NM. I continued to battle El Paso drivers—many of whom seemed completely indifferent to the potential effect of the wind on their vehicles or mine. The open space between El Paso and Las Cruces finally brought traffic relief and sharply colder air. By the time I pulled into the Las Cruces Hilton, I was chilled and ready to be off the bike.

Pre-Christmas parties filled the hotel's function rooms, but a gorgeous room with a view of the majestic Organ Mountains was available for only $69. I knew I had found a home for the night. With Eli carefully covered and shielded from the continuing wind, I set his alarm, shouldered my luggage, and trudged up the hill from the parking lot to the lobby and my room. I was out of Texas and was now one state—and time zone—closer to home.

Pre-Trip Preparation: Hotels and Credit Cards

PREP

Two important subjects to think about before leaving home are where you will spend your nights and how you will pay for them. Even if you choose to camp or plan your stops to stay with family and friends, you may still end up in a hotel one night.[1] And, you'll always need to pay for food, gas, and incidentals along the way.

Hotels and motels

Based on my rides, I suggest that every three or four days, you check into a full-service hotel offering room service, well-equipped bathrooms, and laundry service, if you need it.[2] My stop at the Las Cruces Hilton provided a relaxing break midway through the trip, after a difficult day in wind, dust, and sand. Riding 392 miles doesn't sound tough, particularly after covering 1,099 miles the first day. But battling wind and breathing dirt takes its toll.

---

[1] On my August trip, I planned my route to stay with friends or family on three of the six nights. These stops saved money and added pleasant breaks. Because weather dictated my December route, I was unable to make similar stops on that trip, but learned valuable lessons about lodging.

[2] Laundromats are obviously cheaper, but can be difficult to find while en route. Other riders prefer to bring easy-wash clothing made of synthetic fabrics that can be dried overnight, hanging on a shower curtain rod or improvised clothes line.

View from the Las Cruces Hilton

So, when you budget for your trip, plan at least one hotel splurge somewhere around the middle of your trip, in both directions. When I chose not to camp, I decided to economize whenever possible by choosing inexpensive motels.

For the most part, that was a good, decision. However, although perfectly good motel rooms are available for $30–50 dollars, you'll seldom get much more than a room. And not all rooms in the $30–50 price range are even comfortable. Cranky heating and cooling and no ability to open the windows to get fresh air, headed my complaint list. Cleanliness also varies significantly. I never actually had to turn down a room, but I did remove some well-used blankets from a few of the beds. Finally, weak showers with clingy shower curtains, and tubs with no elbowroom, are closer to the rule than the exception.

Now, before you say, "I can't believe you couldn't find a decent room for $30–50," let's be clear about what I mean by decent. That way, you'll know how your preferences compare to mine and will be able to identify your needs. When I stop at night, I like to have:

- A good shower
- A clean room
- Crisp sheets, a clean blanket, and carpet I'm not afraid to walk on with bare feet
- Windows that open to allow fresh air
- Adequate lighting and security, for me *and* the bike

That's it. And that doesn't seem an unreasonable list. As a business traveler, I've stayed in a lot of very nice hotels—but those were not my standard for this trip. In fact, too often, such hotels are more pretentious than comfortable. I was hoping for down-to-earth, hospitality-for-real-people on this trip.

Still, I tried to remember endurance rider Dave Barr,[3] who spent most nights beside the road and in motorcycle shops. My $30–50 rooms would have been a luxury for him. And an avid camper would probably be overjoyed just not to have to set up a tent and have hot running water and a soft bed. But think about what *you* will need to make your continent crossing a pleasure, not a gut-it-out endurance contest. One other point to keep in mind about camping is the time it takes to find a campground, make camp, and then break it down the next morning. One reason I chose not to camp was the extra time required.

And, if you aren't already a member of a hotel chain's frequent traveler club, join one before you go. All chains list their locations, either on the Internet or in a printed directory you can obtain at any hotel near you. Choose a chain, check for inns along your route, and start accumulating points to use next time.

---

[3] Barr, *Riding the Edge.*

Credit and debit cards

A word about using credit cards on your trip may be helpful. There are many advantages to doing so, including not having to carry or get cash, having a record of your transactions, and earning points for any number of rewards. In fact, if you plan to use credit cards, you should have a couple different types along, just in case a gas station or hotel doesn't take your preferred card (such as American Express or Discover). As you use credit cards, be aware of a couple of special hazards in making a motorcycle trip.

First, as a way of preventing fraudulent use, most credit card companies watch for unusual patterns of use on their accounts. American Express probably is the best or the worst about this, depending on how their scrutiny affects you. For example, about two days into my August trip, Susan received a call from Amex asking if we knew someone was making frequent charges to our account throughout the Western states.

These charges, of course, were gas stops. Since Susan was home and could explain what was going on, no problem resulted from Amex monitoring our account (and they didn't question the same pattern during my December trip). But what would have happened if they had not been able to reach someone? It's likely they would have put a hold on the account. You don't want that somewhere in the dark, when you're running low on cash and it's the last gas station or hotel within miles. Before starting out, you should alert your credit card company (or companies) so they can note the record and approve expected charges.

Another potential credit hazard is pump authorizations when you fill up your tank. I always pay at the pump. This is the quickest and most convenient way to keep moving. But when a transaction is authorized at the pump, the station puts a hold on a certain amount of credit to ensure they'll be paid when transactions on the account are settled (usually overnight). Stations do this because, at the time you insert your card, neither the pump nor the computer it is talking to know whether you're riding a motorcycle with a five-gallon tank—or driving an RV that might hold a hundred or more gallons.

Fair enough. What makes this tricky, however, is the *amount* of the hold varies from station to station. Many gas stations put an average hold on your card of, say, $20 or $30. And while the policy makes sense, most bikes can't hold that much gas. So, after you've made five or six stops, you could have as much as $150–200 tied up in credit holds. If the card you are using is close to its credit limit, these holds could result in authorization being denied later in the day, even if you know your actual charges are are well within your credit limit.

As bad as that may be, using your ATM or debit card for gas can be even worse. The pump puts the same hold on your funds, but now the hold is on the cash in your checking account. Even if you normally keep several hundred dollars in your account, this hold on your cash could cause a transaction to be denied, such as getting cash at an ATM or paying for a meal with your debit card.

Thankfully, I didn't encounter any of these problems and Susan was home when American Express called. But it's good to know these things happen and to be prepared before you start your trip.

EQUIP

Your Equipment:
Cameras

You may have noticed I haven't said much about cameras other than, if you carry one, you should find an exterior pocket in your bike luggage that allows you to reach it conveniently. However, skipping any discussion of cameras for a trip as important as your cross-continent motorcycle journey would be wrong. Don't come home without taking some shots to help you remember what a good time you had. But, since your camera is not officially a part of your bike, I've saved this section until now.

What to take? I'm going to offer my photo prejudices here, based on three recent cross-country trips and three decades of photographic experience. Your choices may differ.

If your trip is primarily about photography, carefully consider your photographic needs in light of the luggage you select. For me, serious photography would require a 35 mm single lens reflex camera body, a decent tripod, and at least a couple of lenses. That's almost impossible to carry on a bike even if you're an enthusiastic photographer. Equally important, with the intent to use that kind of gear, you are also probably considering frequent stops. Nothing wrong with that, but you won't be making a quick trip across the U.S. Plan accordingly.

It's more likely, however, that even serious photographers will choose a smaller camera that can be stuffed in a luggage pocket or jacket. Packing this way helps ensure you actually *use* the camera, rather than just carrying it (which is what will happen if it's stuck somewhere deep in your luggage).

On that basis, here are five factors—in order of importance— for making your choice:

Age of the camera

It may seem strange to say that the age of your camera is the most important factor to consider, but here's why. Over several thousand miles of motorcycle travel, everything you bring is going to be subject to vibration. The amount of vibration depends on your bike and where you carry the camera. Still, no ride is easy for sensitive equipment. Small screws may vibrate out. Dust and dirt are more prevalent than at home or in an automobile. I am not recommending you abuse the camera or misuse manufacturers' warranty privileges. But on two of my three cross-country trips, I returned with a camera needing repair. If you can afford to buy a camera for the trip, choose the best you can, designed for the job, and then expect the manufacturer to back their durability claims if you have problems.

Size of the camera

The smaller the camera is, generally speaking, the more useful it will be. Since your purpose for bringing a camera is to take pictures, buy or bring the smallest you can afford. Without slighting many other fine brands available, if I could choose only one camera for my next trip, it would be the Canon Elph or something very much like it. Models and prices in this series change frequently, so shop for yourself. But these little cameras are smaller than a pack of cigarettes, available in either digital or APS (Advanced Photo System film), and have a built-in zoom lens with cover and flash. The other big advantage of the Elph and similar cameras is that they are almost perfectly smooth outside. Their absence of knobs, levers, and controls makes sliding one into your pocket or into your luggage easier and more trouble free. Even being careful, I've broken small controls off the sides of poorly designed pocket cameras.

Zoom or single focal length lens

Get a zoom. Most of the shots you'll want to take from the road will look better using a telephoto lens. Wide-angle shots almost always show nothing but road and sky ("Oh, are those *mountains* in the distance?").

Digital or conventional film

This is totally a matter of your preference. You can get prints from either. I worry about losing rolls of film en route, until I reach a place to get them developed. So, I prefer a digital camera with lots of memory. Digital preview features also allow you to be certain you got a good shot, before you leave a place you may not visit again soon. And digital photos allow you to easily share parts of your trip with friends and family through email and the Web.

Consider video

Now we're talking bucks and major luggage space. I took a miniature Sony digital video camera on my first cross-country trip. Would I do it again? Probably not, although my family enjoyed the ability to "be there" with me on parts of the trip. Your choice depends on how much you value sound, motion, and the ability to narrate your shots. If you are headed for Sturgis or another motorcycle gathering where you expect sound and motion to be a major feature, bring a video recorder. Otherwise, think stills.

Riding Techniques: Winning Against the Wind

RIDE

When I suited up in Ozona and the wind blew my gloves off Eli and halfway across the parking lot, I knew this was going to be a long day. Wind, even without sand or dust, can test your riding skills and your endurance like almost nothing else.

I have never found a way to make riding in the wind pleasant, but I have learned ways to make riding on windy days safer. You may not be surprised to learn, once again, the most important technique is to maintain your bubble. When riding in the wind, you'll find it even more important to maintain separation from traffic—front, back, and particularly to your sides—because a strong wind can push your bike farther than you might imagine.

Here's an example. All riders hear their share of "Oh, you bought a motorcycle?" stories. You know the type. These stories are the ones told to you by well-meaning friends and family, in hopes of either scaring you off the bike or convincing you to ride carefully—I'm never certain which. But this story about wind made an impression. A friend of a friend ended up in the hospital. He was riding a big road bike when the accident happened. By reputation, he was a very experienced rider. Nevertheless, riding in highway traffic a strong gust of wind blew him into a tractor-trailer truck.

Frankly, I had doubts about the truthfulness of this story until riding across West Texas today. No more. Respect the wind! There were times today when the wind simply *blew me into the next lane*. It wasn't as if I were not trying to maintain lane position. The wind moved me 6–10 feet to the left, despite all I could do. If you don't maintain your bubble, if you don't maintain adequate separation from traffic, that lane may be occupied by something much bigger and heavier than you are.

Be especially careful, too, when riding in changing terrain. What is changing terrain? It may be bluffs beside the highway, where the road has been cut through a hill; it may be a large stand of trees beside the road, in an otherwise flat prairie; it could even be tall or odd-shaped buildings lining the freeway—anything that can block the wind, temporarily changing its effect on your bike.

Changing terrain causes unpredictable wind shifts

Changing terrain can produce wind shear, an abrupt change in the speed or direction of the wind. Wind shear has brought down heavy airliners on approach for landing. An abrupt change in the speed or direction of the wind on the road can do the same to you.

In addition to maintaining your bubble, always have hungry eyes for wind clues. You'll learn to hate stiff roadside foliage that gives you no clue about the wind's direction or strength. You'll rejoice when you see tall grass, flags, or smoke, because they immediately provide clues about the direction, strength, and gustiness of the wind.

Finally, along with your bubble and knowledge of wind direction, keep in mind the "windage" of your bike. How much side area is exposed to the wind? How much exposed surface area is up high (you are; what else?). Do you have wire wheels or discs? Disc wheels are wonderful, because they allow us to run tubeless tires and may give us a few extra seconds in the case of a flat (a tube tire on a spoked wheel will lose all its air through the spoke holes). But discs provide more side area for the wind to work on. And don't forget your luggage. The more luggage you have piled up high behind you, the more windage you've exposed to your enemy—the wind—and the less agile your bike will be in combating this enemy.

Staying Organized: Keeping Your Promises

This section could be called either "Keeping Your Promises," or "Keeping in Touch." You see, I had promised my wife, particularly on my first trip, to phone regularly from fuel stops. Keeping in touch would allow her to track my progress and know that I was safe.

But good intentions don't count for much if you don't follow through. At one point during my summer U.S. crossing, when a call was long overdue, Susan was within minutes of calling the Wyoming state police to ask if I had been in an accident. This incident ranked right up there with the night the FAA[4] phoned her, when I was learning to fly, to say I hadn't arrived at the destination on time and to ask if she knew whether or not my plane had landed safely?

On the second trip, we had a looser agreement that I would call when I could. This plan allowed me flexibility in moving out of a gas stop fast, if I was trying to outrun a storm, for instance. It also provided leeway when I had put on all my gear—helmet, earplugs, neck gaiter—and then remembered I hadn't phoned. As long as Susan knew I might not be able to call, she didn't worry.

So, think of communication with your home base both as a responsibility and an opportunity. You have the responsibility to reassure those you love that you're OK. At the same time, you may have the opportunity to ask for their help when needed. Let's say your bike has developed a funny noise. Someone at home may be able to make several calls to locate a dealership, more easily than you can. Or, as reported in Chapter 9 about riding a SaddleSore 1,000, you may be able to get help with directions, distances, or lodging possibilities when the information you have with you isn't enough. Just remember, as I learned from Susan's cold, to ask first "How are you doing?" before launching into your request.

Take a picture, send a postcard, or make a call. All of these pay dividends with the folks back home, in terms of reassuring them you're doing well and having fun. After all, that's little enough to ask, isn't it? You're the one enjoying the trip, crossing America.

---

[4] The Federal Aviation Administration monitors all flight plans, in order to begin timely search-and-rescue operations when a plane goes down. This event was my first night flight with an instructor, for which we filed a flight plan but forgot to close upon landing. When the FAA learned it was a training flight, they apologized for having caused concern; apparently this was a regrettable, but not uncommon situation.

Thoughts from the Road:
A Happy Toad

Early in the 1990s, a group called TLC recorded a song called "Waterfalls." The lyric of the song underscores the kind of thinking or pressure from others that keeps some of us from making the ride of our dreams:

> *Don't go chasin' waterfalls,*
> *just stick to the rivers and the lakes you're used to.*
> *I know you're gonna have it your way or nothin' at all,*
> *but I think you're movin' too fast.*[5]

When those we love question our trip plans ("Don't go chasin' waterfalls"), or when we're tired or cold, or even when we ourselves are apprehensive about beginning, it's hard to remember a long trip is supposed to be *fun*; a long trip represents freedom and time to think.

Thankfully, everyone who rides long distances seems to have—or perhaps gains along the way—something within that sustains us through the difficult moments. I've come to believe that some part of every distance rider is truly a "Toad."

Kenneth Grahame's book, *Wind in the Willows*, spawned the irascible character that became the basis for "Toad's Wild Ride" at Disney theme parks. You see, Toad has quite a fondness for things

---

[5] "Waterfalls." Words and Music by Marqueze Etheridge, Lisa Nicole Lopes, Rico R. Wade, Pat Brown and Ramon Murray © 1994 EMI APRIL MUSIC INC., BELT STAR MUSIC, PEBBITONE MUSIC, TIZBIZ MUSIC, STIFF SHIRT MUSIC, INC. and ORGANIZED NOIZE MUSIC

All Rights for BELT STAR MUSIC Controlled and Administered by EMI APRIL MUSIC INC.

All Rights for TIZBIZ MUSIC Administered by PEBBITONE MUSIC

All Rights for ORGANIZED NOIZE MUSIC Controlled and Administered by STIFF SHIRT MUSIC, INC.

All Rights Reserved International Copyright Secured Used by Permission

motorized. And what motorcyclist wouldn't echo Toad's sentiments, as he thought about the glories of the open road:

> *"There you are!" cried out Toad…. "There's real life for you…the open road, the dusty highway…here today, up and off to somewhere else tomorrow! Travel, change, interest, excitement! The whole world before you, and a horizon that's always changing!"*[6]

There are certainly easier ways to cross the country than on a motorcycle. But I suspect the self-imposed challenge such a trip involves is a big part of its attraction. One wonders if Toad might affirm Ernie Gann's idea that "exposure to physical hardship and hazard tend[s] to restore certain lost perspectives."[7] Perhaps, except that Toad also loved his creature comforts like a fine dinner and a soft bed.

I'd enjoyed a horizon that was always changing, and even the dusty roads, for more than two weeks now. It was wonderful. And tonight, in the Las Cruces Hilton, I have all the creature comforts I could ask for.

But I know that in the morning, packing my gear and starting the engine, I'll once again become eager to be "up and off to somewhere else—the whole world before me!"

I'm a happy Toad.

---

[6] Kenneth Grahame, *Wind in the Willows* (New York: Aladdin Books, 1989), p. 29. You'll find many editions of *Willows*, but the Henry Holt hardcover edition with Michael Hague's wonderful illustrations is worth the extra cost. You may also enjoy William Horwood's sequels. As an admirer of Toad and his friends, Horwood continued the series after Grahame's death. Look for *The Willows in Winter* and *Toad Triumphant*, published by St. Martin's Press (New York).
[7] Gann, *Song of the Sirens*, p. 21.

Things that make toads happy

Chapter 12:

A Brand New Day

Sunday, December 22
Las Cruces, NM to Goodyear, AZ—406 Miles

TRIP

The Trip:
Throw Off the Bowlines

As I savored breakfast in my room at the Las Cruces Hilton, I considered the rest of the trip. Depending on weather and traffic, I could be home in three days, maybe two. Packing the bike, I thought, "Just see how it goes. It would be great to be home early, but don't push beyond what's sensible." Still it was hard not to be optimistic. The sun was out. The bike was warming up. I'd had a great night's rest. What a glorious day and what a wonderful trip!

Mark Twain said:

Twenty years from now you will be more disappointed in the things you didn't do than by the ones you did do. So throw off the bowlines. Sail away from the safe harbor. Catch the tradewinds in your sails. Explore... Dream... Discover...[1]

---

[1] Mark Twain (1835-1910), American writer and humorist.

Twain was right. I'm convinced years from now we *will* be more disappointed in the things we didn't do than by the things we did. While caught up in the busy-ness of our 21ˢᵗ century lives, we still must not continually postpone our dreams.

The miles passed quickly today. Retracing the route I'd ridden 14 days ago across New Mexico and Arizona seemed almost effortless. Part of the ease stemmed from the absence of the wind that plagued my eastbound trip, and even yesterday's ride. But a more important reason the miles just seemed to fall away today was contentment. The trip was nearly over. The bike was running well. Home was within reach. The journey had been a wonderful experience.

As the miles passed, I realized Eli expresses himself in different ways at different speeds. Around town, he lopes. His engine's low-end torque is strong enough that idling along in almost any gear is possible. At road speeds, however, his personality changes. At 55, he cruises. At 65 mph, he pounds. For whatever reason, at 65 the semi-vertical pounding in the big twin seems greater than at any other speed. But at 75 mph, Eli purrs. At this speed, his engine is almost turbine-smooth. We rolled through much of New Mexico and Arizona like a turbine at the speed limit.

Saw another solo rider headed east on I-10. Waved, as I always do. This rider didn't look lonely, in contrast to another rider I had noticed when I was eastbound. I wondered if my interpretation of other riders' feelings depended on my direction of travel? Did the rider today look happier because I was headed home? Because the trip was almost complete?

Passing through Tucson, I silently saluted the guys who'd gotten Eli in and out of service quickly after the sand storm. Most brands have a pretty solid fraternity of riders and dealers. It would be interesting to do this trip again, but on a BMW K1200. BMW riders seem as fanatically loyal to their marques as Harley owners.

Might be fun on a Honda 1800 mega V-twin, too, or even on the new 1800 cc Gold Wing. My meditation on which bike to use for my next trip was interrupted, however, by shocking pink guardrails near Rillita Creek in Tucson. I guess Texas, doesn't have a monopoly on the color pink.

Approaching Phoenix I decided to go beyond downtown and stay on the west side of town. Traffic through town was light since it was Sunday and the express lane was nearly empty. It was a quick trip out to Goodyear, AZ, where I stopped, fearing that choices would be fairly limited farther beyond.

Dusk was falling as I pulled into the Hampton Inn, Goodyear. After tucking Eli into his cover, I walked across the street to Stuart Anderson's Black Angus for a beer and a steak, and then tucked myself in for the night.

What's left—a day, two at most? Just rest up to ride. See what the morning brings.

Pre-Trip Preparation: Deciding to Go

PREP Nothing can really prepare you for the most important step in making a long motorcycle trip. The first and most important step is simply deciding to go. The most important "thing" to prepare is *you*. You have to carve out time to make the journey and that's difficult in the types of lives most of us lead.

So many of us (me included) spent years as career machines instead of human beings. Maybe Sting's U.S. performance of "A Brand New Day," at the turn of the year 2000, should be thought of as a re-declaration of personal independence for some of us.

Challenger, Gray, & Christmas—a job placement firm—reports Americans are increasingly scouting for work close to home. Just "14% of job seekers relocated for new jobs during the first quarter of 2002, down sharply from previous years."[2] We're no longer willing to uproot our lives just for a company. Similarly, in Japan, a government-published *Lifestyle White Paper* publicly lambasted "18-hour work days and mandatory drinks with the boss," with the goal being to "free people from Japan's corporate grind . . . so they can better balance family and career."[3]

And without abandoning their responsibilities, more and more people are deciding to focus on their families, simplify their lives, or retire while they are healthy enough to realize their deferred dreams. Kent Sherwood, the CEO of Sutter Medical, retired in early 2002 to pursue his passion for mountain climbing.[4] Later the same year, Karen Hughes left the center of power in Washington, D.C., for Texas, to focus on her family. Even closer to home, most of us actually know someone—often *more than one* person—who has done the same thing.

Think about your motorcycle journey as a chance to recalibrate life. Remember Clement Salvadori's words that put me on the road: "This is your moment of opportunity, your chance to slip through the door of everyday constraints and out into the wide world. Do it! Don't even finish reading this; put on the jacket and boots and the helmet and get out there. Now! Quick!"[5]

Go ride. Just ride.

Your Equipment: Earplugs

EQUIP

Your miles will be more pleasant, as mine were today, if you take along two of the smallest—but most useful—

---

[2] Hebert B. Herring, "Scouting for Work, but Close to the Nest," *The New York Times*, April 28, 2002.

[3] Hans Greimel, "Japan Urges Young People to Work Less, Have More Babies," *The Press Democrat* (Associated Press), March 27, 2002.

[4] Bleys W. Rose, "Sutter CEO in SR to Step Down," *The Press Democrat*, April 20, 2002.

[5] Salvadori, "Overcoming Inertia."

pieces of equipment you can acquire: good earplugs. Since they can make a huge difference in riding comfort and lack of fatigue at the end of the day, earplugs deserve attention before the close of the trip.

I haven't yet found the ideal earplugs. Different types of earplugs are made for various applications, from water sports (mostly to keep water from entering the ear canal) to industrial safety (with applications as diverse as working in manufacturing to performing in a rock group). Here are some thoughts on choosing from among the many options.

Custom-fitted earplugs

Ideally, earplugs should be custom fitted. You can visit an audiologist for this work. Or, sometimes it is possible to have earplugs made for you at gun shows or the larger motorcycle gatherings. However, I've had no luck at two successive HOG rallies, nor at Street Vibrations in Reno. So, you may have to find a local provider. HearUSA maintains a nice online site, including a provider directory of audiologists.[6] Just go to the site, click the "Provider Directory" link and enter your ZIP code for a list of audiologists within a specified radius of your home.

Off-the-shelf earplugs

If you choose not to have earplugs fitted, scan motorcycle magazines or search the Web using Google[7] for a list of earplug suppliers. Web product availability changes, but the day I made a quick search, several sites offered acceptable types of mass-produced plugs. What makes an earplug acceptable?

---

[6] See *www.hearusa.com*.

[7] I've found Google consistently returns more useful results, from a simpler user interface, than Yahoo and competing search engines. Try *www.google.com*.

Intended function

Choose plugs designed for noise reduction. The higher the noise reduction rating (NRR) number, the more likely you are to be satisfied. My experience has proven you still hear traffic, horns, sirens, and so forth, to an adequate degree, but the constant wind noise and the overwhelming racket of nearby traffic—particularly large trucks—is significantly reduced.

Material

The material the earplugs are made from depends, in part, on their intended use. For example, many earplugs designed for water sports are made of silicone. While silicone may be a fine choice, it's not necessary for noise reduction if you don't also have to contend with water. Some of the best plugs I've used were inexpensive soft foam that simply conformed to the shape of my ear canal, after being compressed and inserted.

Design

Choose plugs designed for *constant* noise reduction. One of the least successful pairs of earplugs I've tried were designed to block the sound of a gun being fired, but to admit normal sounds. This particular set of plugs featured a triple-flange design that is also sometimes used to enhance the fit of swimmer's earplugs. Avoid this design for best noise reduction.

Corded or non-corded

Some riders prefer to have earplugs tethered to a cord so when they remove them, the cord dangles around their necks and their plugs are less easily misplaced. While admitting the good sense of this approach (as well as the fact I've lost a handful of earplugs), the extra expense and reduced selection may make corded earplugs a less desirable solution for you.

RIDE

Riding Techniques:
Ten More Ways to Stay Safe

As I came close to finishing roughly 10,000 miles of riding, I thought about what techniques had been most valuable. In addition to the "Ten Ways to Stay Safe" in Chapter 8, here are 10 more to round out the list and make you the best rider possible on your next trip.

1. Scan, scan, scan.

Assuming you have enough skill to keep your motorcycle upright in most situations, *maintaining situational awareness—*knowing what's going on around your motorcycle—is the most important technique you can develop. Put your eyeballs on stalks, like a space creature, and constantly scan to the front, to the rear (in your mirrors), and to both sides. A more complete treatment of this topic appears in Chapter 2.

2. Be prickly!

This expression was used in Chapter 8 as shorthand for making certain you become and remain visible to the traffic around you. Do whatever it takes to be noticed. The most common excuse after a motorcycle crash involving another vehicle—car, truck, even another motorcyclist perhaps—is, "But I never saw him/her!" Use your bright lights, turn signals and emergency flashers, lane position, bright colored or reflective clothing, even attention-getting movement like controlled weaving. Put an American flag waving from your bike! Whatever it takes to be noticed, do it. And don't hesitate to use hand signals. If you saw the film *Patton*, think of the scene in which Patton's tanks couldn't advance because of a vehicle ahead mired in the mud. Patton jumped out and began directing traffic until his men were on the move again. Do the same with motorists around you. Be sure they know what you need and what you intend to do next.

3. Learn to slide.

There are many ways to learn this technique, from growing up on dirt bikes to attending Danny Walker's American Supercamp. But learn it. The combination of braking and bike-handling may be exactly what you need to get out of a tight spot somewhere along the road. For the purposes of keeping the "Top Ten" down to just ten techniques, I'll include emergency braking here. Know what your bike will do when you need full stoppers. Know how to slide, just in case you need even more than stopping power. Discussion of these techniques appears in Chapter 10, "Riding Techniques."

4. Watch the wind.

Of all the weather conditions that can affect a motorcyclist, wind is the most difficult. Part of the reason is the wind's effect changes, depending on whether it is steady or gusty, what the terrain around you is like, how close you are to other traffic, and more. It's no fun, but on the next howling day in your part of the country, get out and practice. See Chapter 11 for more on this technique. There are some things you don't want to learn the hard way during your ride.

5. Beware of trucks.

Truckers don't have any special animosity toward motorcyclists. In fact, many long-haul drivers are also riders and most of them show great courtesy when maneuvering around you and your bike. But trucks' sheer size and weight makes them dangerous. Following, overtaking and passing them, and being aware of special dangers (like disintegrating tires) all require special care. Chapter 5 discusses this subject more fully.

6. Pass skillfully.

Every passing situation generates a different threat to you and your bike. Limited access interstate highways pose challenges unlike two-lane highways. Oncoming trucks generate wind turbulence different from trucks traveling in the same direction as you. Wind adds a variable in any of these situations. The most important fact to keep in mind is, while passing, your bubble of separation has been penetrated by another vehicle. Use the extra caution that change deserves! See Chapter 6 for some specific tips.

7. Use lane position strategically.

Unlike an automobile, a motorcycle is not locked into one position within the lane. The motorcyclist has at least three paths (left, right, and center) within the lane. Each has its advantages, depending on the circumstances. When you are on a multilane road, ride in either the outermost (right hand) or innermost (far left hand) lanes. Doing so eliminates half the threats around you—the cars or trucks beside you—and opens up the shoulder as an escape. But be cautious about oil and automobile droppings in the center portion of any lane. See Chapter 7.

8. Load your bike carefully.

Motorcycles are exceptionally forgiving with respect to weight and balance. Under normal circumstances, you can probably ride most bikes even when they are badly loaded. Problems occur when the circumstances become anything less than "normal." A sudden turn, forceful braking, or strong winds can all affect a badly loaded bike—turning it, potentially, into a lethal vehicle. Know your maximum tire loads, observe any rack restrictions, and be sure to secure any non-factory bags or luggage well. Chapter 1 spends a significant amount of time on this topic.

9. Watch yourself systematically.

As riders, we must always be sure we, as well as our bikes, are in condition to travel safely. Pilots sometimes use as a mental checklist: "I'M SAFE." It works for motorcyclists, too:

I   =   Illness?

M =   Medication, which would affect your concentration or safety?

S   =   Stress, which would prevent you from focusing, scanning?

A   =   Alcohol?

F   =   Fatigue?

E   =   Equipment, inspected, serviced, adequately prepared?

10. Have fun, every single day of the trip!

If you aren't having fun, there's no point being on the road. Sure, some days go better than others. But there was not a single day I wasn't pleased to run a hand over the nice lines of my bike in the mornings; happy to hear its engine come to life; and grinning from ear-to-ear when I rolled on the power and pulled out of the motel parking lot. If you're a rider, you know what I mean. Your trip should be a joy. If something happens to turn it into drudgery, take a break. If things don't get better, ship the bike home. Don't lose your joy of riding. Take a step back and start planning your *next* trip.

A Few Last Thoughts from the Road

I'll be home soon. Time to return to "normal" life. There are parts of that life I am very much looking forward to resuming: the joys of the Christmas season; time with family; even the routine activities of day-to-day life, from showering to shopping. These are things altered or omitted on the road.

Yet, it is impossible to forget that many other dimensions of everyday life can be less pleasant, even onerous. We live in a world that often wears us down in purposeless activity, and then seeks to revive us through compulsive escape.

The modern reduction of all human action to servile labor...from executive to machine tender...uses men [and women].[8]

Doubt this assessment? Then ask the average worker—from factory floor machine operator to corporate executive—what purpose they find in their work? What noble end does it serve? Ask whether they would continue doing the same work, if they had the financial means to quit? Sadly, too many would answer, "No. No purpose, no clear end worth achieving, and no way I'd continue if I didn't need a paycheck." Are your answers to these questions much different?

In our often purposeless work, as well as in our equally frantic attempts to convince ourselves our earnings have bought the good life, no space remains for *true* leisure: for time with family and friends, for time alone, for quiet, contemplative thought. It is ironic that some of us find quiet time on long rides with very loud pipes. Let those pipes call us to better lives.

"Loud pipes save lives" is widely disputed in the motorcycling community. But perhaps we've misunderstood. Perhaps our application of the thought has been too limited. Is it possible that the goal of our pipes is not to call attention to our physical presence in traffic? No, the more important saving of lives is the pipes' call to *live* life, to come apart from the work-a-day world and *find* life.

---

[8] Josef Pieper. *Leisure: The Basis of Culture.* (South Bend, IN: St. Augustine's Press, Inc., 1998) p. 148. This work was originally published in 1948 by Kösel-Verlag in Germany.

As the reality of getting closer to home sinks in, a wonderful peace surrounds me. It's clear, even when we must return to the demands of daily life, a long ride—a crossing of America—can restore perspective; recharge our batteries, so we can face the demands of that life with a new degree of calm and balance.

Are the demands of our work unimportant? Absolutely not! In fact, with the perspective gained from two or three weeks away, our goal may well be to return to work, clear about what next—rather than ceaselessly laboring to no apparent end. As we find our rides have changed us, we may also decide to change our work. Or, finding our rides have clarified what is important to us, we may decide to change our approach to work—to bring to work each day a sense of craft that will not be hurried; will not be bullied by production demands; will not be overwhelmed by the pressures of quarterly earnings reports, but will insist on doing the right things, the right way, at the right time.

Are our responsibilities to our families and friends unimportant? In no way! But with the mental and emotional space gained from riding alone, our objective should be to return to families and friends refreshed, able to appreciate all we have—rather than constantly dwelling on what we do not have. Single or married, supporting children or supporting parents, a broad circle of friends or just a few, we should return better able to recognize their needs and the dreams of those around us. We should now encourage them to pursue their dreams and support them in doing it

But first, *we* must make time. We must create *true* leisure. We must set that time apart.

We must ride. Just ride. Just go

Chapter 13:

Turn of the Wheel
Monday, December 23
Goodyear, AZ to Santa Rosa, CA—862 Miles

The Trip:
Run at Dawn to Run Fast

Monday morning in Goodyear, I awakened early, just before sunrise. Seeing the weather appeared perfect for a final, one-day push to Santa Rosa, I packed the bike and fired up the engine. Just as he had every other morning of the trip, Eli responded willingly. Soon, the happy warmth of his engine began to drift up and warm my hands in the chilly pre-dawn air. We were ready to go! My friend and I were ready for the last lap.

The remainder of Arizona flew by, gorgeous in the low, early morning sunlight. All the miles I've ridden since August have been enough to convince me there are "speed grooves"—zones riders can enter, in which the miles just fall away effortlessly. I'd had my share of bad days getting out of California early in this trip. Today redeemed all of that. Without consciously riding differently or more rapidly, I fell into the groove almost immediately after leaving the Hampton Inn. The road surface was great. I'd had a good rest and a full breakfast (hot buffet with abundant choices, all included in the price of the Hampton Inn, Goodyear).

Maybe the knowledge gained from this early morning Arizona-to-California leg is something like "run at dawn to run fast." Wind was nonexistent. Traffic was light. Although this morning's ride bucked my biological clock, which would prefer to ride late into the night, today worked. The California state line came into view quickly. I wished I had remembered to stop short of the line for fuel. Prices in Blythe were significantly higher than those in Arizona, perhaps as much as $0.50 per gallon.

The Los Angeles smog began around Indio, barely 100 miles into California. Apparently, wind through the San Gorgonio Pass was carrying the smog this direction today. Palm Springs and the mountains between the desert and L.A. were totally obscured. The whole area looked like "after the bomb." Buildings were still standing, but a horrible haze clouded the area and metal cockroaches were dashing about everywhere.

In light of this buttermilk-thick air, it seems remarkable I saw only one electric or hybrid car during my trips through the edges of Los Angeles. The Los Angeles basin must have been beautiful when originally settled. The mountains to the east, the ocean to the west—truly it must have seemed "the city of angels." One would think the pollution might be self-regulating. As the air became brown and obscured the natural beauty of the area, people would have moved away, reducing the traffic and the pollution. But sadly, it hasn't worked that way.

Electric vehicles and public transportation simply should be required. It would be generations, perhaps, before the beauty of the city returned. But what a waste, particularly as our cars inflict similar damage in San Diego, Salt Lake City, the Front Range from Colorado Springs to Boulder, and innumerable cities elsewhere. The air I'm riding through today is insane. As much as I love the throb of Eli's big twin, I'd gladly board an electric train to be ferried through the L.A. area, if the cities and counties of the basin had the courage to roll back the clock on pollution.

Katie Alvord writes, "Worldwide in the 1990s, the number of cars grew three times faster than the human population. Vehicles have gotten bigger, too. Cars have encouraged developed areas to sprawl at up to ten times the rate of population growth in U.S. cities. Cars also consume expanding amounts of time. On average, we spend over one hour a day in the car and, in places like Los Angeles, perhaps double that. [We are a] drive-by society."[1] Somehow, we must learn from the lessons of Los Angeles. This is not an issue of politics or personal sacrifice. This is essential to preserve any reasonable quality of life.[2]

Highway 395 led me away from L.A. and back into the desert. It was a welcome change. In addition to the clear air, I knew the road was taking me to the Roadhouse Restaurant and Bakery at Four Corners (Highways 58 and 395 in Kramer Junction, CA) for a repeat of the wonderful meal I'd had traveling eastbound. I pulled into their parking lot just in time for a late lunch and repeated my order for a three-egg Spanish omelet. I wasn't disappointed.

Back on the bike. Crossing the Mojave Desert next to Edwards Air Force Base and entering the town of Mojave, I passed dozens of mothballed airliners sitting idle in the dry air. While not as extensive as the collection of military planes stored in Tucson at Davis-Monthan, the airliners here were somehow more poignant. With their vertical stabilizers silhouetted against the mountains beyond, at a distance they almost looked like a field planted with boomerangs—one side buried in the ground and the sweep of their tails raised skyward, as if pleading to be airborne again. Drivers slowed as they passed. Certainly some were curious. One hopes,

---

[1] Katie Alvord, *Divorce Your Car*. (Gabriola Island, BC: New Society Publishers, 2000), pp. 54-57.
[2] Alvord, *Divorce Your Car*, p. 153.

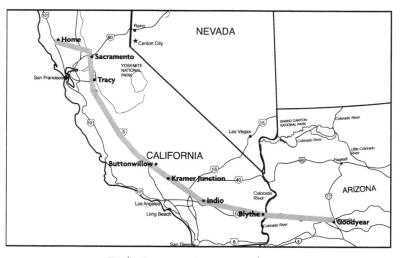

Today's route: Arizona to home

however, that many slowed out of respect for the many hundreds of thousands of miles these aircraft carried their passengers safely. It was sad to see them sitting empty, in the desert.

Eli and I gained altitude to cross the Tehachapi Pass. I glanced backward to the desert. We were ascending into mist and clouds. Despite the beautiful alpine-like scenery of the high meadows around me, I'd miss the desert sunshine. But we were headed for Bakersfield and that meant Santa Rosa was possible by bedtime. With one last regretful glance at the desert, I began the descent down the westbound side of the Pass into California's agricultural central valley.

Bakersfield again. Déjà vu. I pulled off the freeway for gas at the same exit where I'd stayed the first night of the trip. The eight in the Super 8 sign could have been turned sideways to become an infinity sign, representing the sense of returning to that moment. Re-entry into daily life would be a big change after becoming accustomed to the rhythm of the road. But Christmas at home beckoned. Eli accelerated up the ramp and we aimed for a Santa Rosa arrival sometime after nightfall.

Traveling north, smells returned! The fragrances of America had been infrequent during this December journey. But now, the smells of solid agriculture—earth and animals—were apparent. The aroma of a cigar drifting through the open window of the Mercedes in front of me mingled with the fragrance of good earth. A commercial cattle feedlot passed to the east. Home at last, or something very close to it.

Pulling on gloves in the late afternoon after the final gas stop near Tracy, CA, I decided to go through Sacramento and avoid Bay Area commute traffic by not taking I-580 to Highway 101, the obvious route to Sonoma County. In preparation, I mentally rehearsed the route through Sacramento. California's capital city was the last major obstacle between here and Sonoma County's redwoods, rolling hills, and vineyards.

That rehearsal notwithstanding, an hour later Eli and I were neck deep in the worst traffic since rush hour in Atlanta. Apparently everyone in Northern California had decided "to grandmother's house we go" for Christmas—and their route was on I-80 through Sacramento. However, those drivers' holiday spirit was hardly evident. Eli and I experienced some of our most uncomfortable moments of the trip on this stretch of freeway. Was I just tired? I didn't think so. Perhaps I was pushing too hard. Get-home-itis can kill, even during the last hundred miles of a 6,000-mile trip. Pay attention. Scan, scan, scan. Back off and hang out in the far right-hand lane, if you need a breather. No arrival deadline, self-imposed or otherwise, is worth risking injury or death.

After what seemed an interminable amount of time in traffic, I exited onto state Highway 12 to complete the westbound journey. Darkness and quiet returned, punctuated only by Eli's headlight and low exhaust rumble. Napa passed as we rushed through the darkness. We crossed the Sonoma County line. The aromas of pine, eucalyptus, and wood fires greeted us. We were home again, for Christmas—California-style.

After phoning from the road to update my arrival time (not that Susan and the dog wouldn't have recognized the sound of Eli's pipes coming down the street), I rolled into our driveway about 10 p.m.

Arriving at home in Santa Rosa

What can I say about arrival? Dudley barked like crazy, as if I'd never left, just like he'd tried to convince me to stay home three weeks ago. The worry lines melted from my Mom's face as she saw her firstborn return safely from his adventure. And Susan was relieved and happy, not only because of my safe return, but also because I had accomplished what I'd set out to do.

After 6,121 miles this trip—including my rides around town in Greenville—and another 3,400 in August, was I glad to be home? You bet! Yes, I could have made better time. Yes, I should have bypassed Sacramento. Yes, yes, yes. But all the "could haves, should haves" evaporated in the sheer joy of being home. Is this one reason we ride—to appreciate all we have when we return?

Susan and my Mom took arrival photos, and then we unpacked the bike and enjoyed a late-evening snack. The embraces, the talk, and the food were much welcomed after a longer-than-expected day on the road. Our Christmas tree was lit. Packages spilled out in all directions under the tree. The smells of Christmas were in the air: the fragrance of the evergreen tree in our living room, special dishes being prepared just for Christmas, the comfortable aromas of home! I had made it home for Christmas Eve.

Trip Awards: And the Winners Are...

Many events end with an awards ceremony. In that tradition, here are a few of my choices—best and worst—after crossing the U.S. three times in twelve months. Obviously, the categories are not exhaustive, but they are the ones that made the biggest impression while traveling.

Worst Drivers Award

The "Worst Drivers Award" was a hard-fought contest among four cities. Having spots for only three winners, I'll omit El Paso, allowing that perhaps the dust and sand storms contributed to my unpleasant passages through that city. The winners, then.

Third Place: Atlanta, at rush hour

Although Atlanta has finished most of the road construction that dogged the city's growth years and preparation for the 1996 Summer Olympics, negotiating its freeways at night, in the rain, among aggressive drivers, was one of the least pleasant experiences of the trip.

Second Place: Sacramento two days before Christmas

The principal sin of the capital city's drivers was rushing up behind the motorcycle and then braking sharply, as if disappointed Eli and I didn't just vanish. Tailgating with less than a car's-length of separation and veering suddenly into the adjacent lane also helped earn their award.

First Place and Grand Prize: Southern California from San Bernardino to Indio

The Los Angeles area was the winner, since L.A.'s drivers demonstrated—eastbound and westbound—unparalleled indifference to speed limits, crosswind effects, and motorcyclists trying to survive while on the same roadways. I apologize for awarding two of the top three prizes to home-state locations, but trust it's clear affection played no part in my choices.

Friendliest People Award

One might imagine, during the Christmas season, many localities would have contended for this award. Surprisingly, only two areas rose to the awards level, although it should be emphasized I met wonderful individuals at many different places along the route. Two winners share the top spot.

Tie for First Place: West Texas

The people from the Ft. Stockton to Kerrville, as described in Chapter 6, were extraordinarily gracious and helpful. Eli and I send our thanks. The judges trust Texans will excuse any unintended error in labeling a swath that broad as "west" Texas.

Tie for First Place: Greenville, SC

In 1999, Greenville, SC hosted one of the most successful, enjoyable national rallies ever conducted by Harley Owners Group. While visiting my children that summer, we spent two days absorbing the sights and sounds at the HOG Rally.

Two weeks after returning home, Eli was in our garage. So, Greenville and the HOG Rally were the real start of this trip. Thanks, Greenville, for a wonderful time in 1999 and your great hospitality this trip.

Best Road Food Award

Family cooking aside, which was wonderful, and mini-marts, which hardly qualify as food sources, there were two winners in the best road food category.

Second place: Alpine Lodge Restaurant, Ft. Stockton, TX

The Alpine Lodge Restaurant, next door to the Swiss Clock Inn in Ft. Stockton, provided a wonderful start to my day while I was there. Service was prompt, the people were friendly, and the restaurant wasn't overheated—a benefit that's hard to find during the winter in parts of the country where the weather gets cold. Wish I'd been able to try their dinner menu!

First place: Roadhouse Restaurant and Bakery, Kramer Junction, CA

Located at Four Corners (the intersection of Highways 58 and 395 in Kramer Junction, CA), the Roadhouse earned double stops, eastbound and westbound. Their Spanish omelet was worth the stop, any time of day. Don't miss it!

Thoughts from Home

As I drifted off to sleep, happy to be in my own bed again, memories from the trip drifted lazily through my mind. The days and the miles replayed themselves in a sleepy haze. As they did, I realized the trip had been completed in "lumps." I didn't do the consistent 400-500 miles per day I set out to do. Some days I rode as few as 200-300 miles; on others I covered 800 to 1,000 miles or more.

But life is like that. It doesn't come to us evenly. So we live it in lumps—up at times, down at others. Frustrated now, productive tomorrow. We coast along in smooth air for years, but then hit frightening turbulence in a heartbeat.

Would I do the trip again? Absolutely.

But was I happy to be home? You'd better believe it.

And that, too—the joy of being home and the appreciation of how many blessings we have—is part of what making a very long motorcycle journey is about.

Ride well, my friends. Stay safe. But get going.

Ride. Just ride.

Epilogue

The Turn of the Wheel

Chorus *I speak the King's English.*
I kneel in his chapel.
I face forty lashes for stealing his apples.
I'll live in his tavern
Die in his field,
A drink to his health and the turn of the wheel.

Michael's my name, I was born in this clatter.
Twenty-five years, as if nothing's the matter,
It's hard to become very much of a man.
When you've been walking around
With your hat in your hand. *Chorus*

I don't mind the rattle of coin in my pocket,
But I'd sooner buy my dear Rosie a locket,
Than bleed this old countryside, dry to the bone,
Pour me another one
Here's to the throne! *Chorus*

Up on a hill, in a castle of stone,
A withered old monarch lies sleeping alone.
While here at the bar, with my Rose on my knee.
I know which one of us
I'd rather be. *Chorus*

Appendix A:

Pre-Trip Checklist

This appendix suggests items to take on your trip. It is designed to help you as you gather and purchase items, and as a final check while packing your bike.

Your needs will vary based on the activities you plan en route (for example, swimming, email, running, photography) and whether you want a complete change of clothes each day. The time of year you make your trip will also dictate some items, but depending on where you travel, you should be prepared for a variety of climates and weather conditions.

Note: For items with no quantity listed, you'll need to determine an appropriate quantity for your needs and trip length.

In Your Luggage

Qty	Item	Details	Additional Notes
	Garbage bags, Ziploc bags	All sizes. Big bags for lining luggage and packing; gallon and sandwich sizes for organizing and waterproofing	
	Bike cleaning materials	A couple of good-sized rags in plastic bags and plexi cleaner for windscreen	Possibly Armor All Wipes and wash/wax of your choice
	Your preferred reading material	I always take too many	Instead, you may want to take magazines you can read and throw away
	Pen(s), pencil(s), highlighter(s), paper	For taking notes, keeping a journal, or exchanging addresses with people you meet	
	Underclothes	Take as many changes as you expect to need given your planned trip length	
1	Jeans	Evening wear	
1	Toiletries kit	Be sure that you include hand cream, eye drops	
1	Bike cover	Combination of weather protection and theft deterrent	
1	Bike lock or alarm	For protecting your bike from theft and the elements	See page 44 for a longer discussion

1	Flashlight	Be sensible about the size, but make sure it's rugged enough
1	Cell phone battery charger	These are usually small and light
1	Swimsuit	For hotels with hot tubs or pools
1	Tiger Balm	Best soreness aid (akin to Icy Hot, or similar products).
1	E-Z Leaker	An, umm, alternative to rest stops. See page 73 for a longer discussion
2	Helmets	One full-face helmet and one half helmet or shorty. You'll definitely want both in summer. Full-face alone might do in winter.
2	Boot socks (2 pair)	Go to a Western store. I recommend Thor-Lo high-top boot socks. Two pieces are a minimum for 5–7 days. You may want (and have room) for more
2	T-shirts	Gray or black is better about not showing dirt. Two are a minimum for 5–7 days. You may want (and have room) for more
2	Bandanas	Good for covering biker hair, as well as your nose and mouth in dust or sandy conditions
2	Cell phone batteries	Carry a charger, keep one battery fresh while other is in the phone. Keep the phone off when you ride
3	Turtlenecks	These get dirtiest at cuffs and the neck (breathing through them in dusty conditions). Three are a minimum for 5–7 days. You may want (and have room) for more

With You and Accessible

Qty	Item	Details	Additional Notes
	Basic maps for trip route	Get state maps and even a Trip-Tik from AAA/CAA, if you belong	Also carry a dealer list or a manufacturer's atlas that includes a dealer list
	Reflective tape	For making night travel safer (helmet, bags, packs, etc.)	Possibly a reflective joggers vest to tie over your luggage
	Good shoulder strap(s) for your bike bags	Go to a luggage store. Eagle Creek Travel Gear makes good ones	Get strap with padded, rubberized pad for shoulder strap pad
1	Road America card	Roadside assistance and towing	In the event you can't remedy the problem
1	Toolkit for the bike	See Appendix B for contents	
1	Cell phone	For safety and communication with home base	May be cheaper to call home, too, if you have unlimited roaming and free long distance
1	Compact camera	You may want a digital or video camera	Disposable is also an option
1	First aid kit	A commercially-assembled kit made up for backpackers will work	Sawyer Products makes a good kit (see www.sawyerproducts.com)
1	Sailor's watch-type cap or ski cap	Handy for warming your head while unpacking or packing the bike	
2	Neck protectors	Suggest Schampa with yoke, not just neck protector	
2	Gloves (2 pair)	Lightweight, if season permits, plus waterproof and electric	Even in summer, you'll need two pairs (one can get wet)

You'll Be Wearing

Qty	Item	Details	Additional Notes
1	Leather or other protective jacket	I like leather, but there are a lot of materials available	
1	Leather or other protective pants	In summer, jeans work well	
1	Chaps	Chaps give you more layering options than full leathers	
1	Wool tights	Winter trip; you'll probably wear them every day as your first layer	
1	Boots	Be sure you have the best non-slip rubber sole possible!	I prefer combat-style boots, that both lace and zip

You'll Want Handy, in Case of Rain

Qty	Item	Details	Additional Notes
1	Rain jacket	I prefer two piece outfit, with pants having overalls-type bib	Jacket should have reflective material
1	Rain pants	Bib-type is best	
1	Gaiters, for boots	These also provide warmth, on cold dry days	

211

Your Luggage and Packing Supplies

Qty	Item	Details	Additional Notes
	Good bike luggage	Don't get the largest, get the best fitting	Lightweight, good zippers, lots of outside pockets, interlocking D-rings
	Velcro straps in various lengths	As needed	
1	18" two-cord bungee with an O-ring	This allows you to make a neat bungee "X," to secure big items (rather than using two slippery cords)	
1	18" single bungee cord	Obviously, the quantity of bungee cords you carry can vary, depending on what best secures your gear on the bike	
1	24" bungee cord		
3	12" bungee cords		

Appendix B:

Tool Kit Checklist

This appendix suggests items for your tool kit. The specific tools in your kit will vary, as well as U.S. or metric sizes, based on motorcycle brand and any specialty accessories. This kit should work well for most Harleys.

Tools and Supplies

Qty	Item	Details
1	Electrical tape (small roll)	
1	Duct tape (small roll)	Highly recommended by Iron Butt Association riders for fast enroute repairs
1	Wire (small roll)	
1	Assortment of zip ties	Get them at an electronics or computer store, if your auto/motorcycle parts shop doesn't have them
1	Hex keys/allen wrenches (1 set)	Only carry the sizes needed for your bike. I prfer 3/8''' socket driver version for larger hex keys"
1	Torx keys (1 set)	Harley-Davidson uses Torx in a number of places
1	3/8" socket driver to torx converter	
1	1/4" socket driver to torx converter	May not be necessary if you don't need smaller size Torx keys
1	9/16" socket for 3/8" driver	
1	13/16" spark plug socket for 3/8" driver	
1	Spare sparkplugs (1 set)	
1	3/8" socket wrench	
1	6" extension driver for 3/8" socket wrench	

1	3/8" to 1/4" socket converter
1	Deep 5/8" socket
1	T-handle 3/8" driver
1	Feeler gauges (1 set)
1	#2 Phillips screwdriver
1	1/4" flathead screwdriver
1	10 mm open end wrench
1	3/8" and 7/16" open end combination
1	1/2" and 9/16" open end combination
1	5/8" and 3/4" open end combination
1	13 mm and 14 mm open end combination — I purchased this tool at a bicycle shop, because it needed to have an unusually thin cross-section
1	8" crescent wrench
1	Open-jaw pliers (1 pair)
1	Roll-up tool pouch
1	Tubeless tire plug-type repair kit — If you have spoke wheels and tube tires, you'll either need to be a decent mechanic, or call roadside assistance

Other or Different Tools and Supplies (Create Your Own List)

Qty	Item	Details

Appendix C:

Supplier Directory

This appendix lists companies and individuals from whom you can purchase products discussed in this book. Q3 Press has done everything possible to ensure that the information listed in this directory is complete and current, as of the publication date.

In some cases this has required combining information from several sources. Some organizations like the American Motorcyclist Association and Fog City / Modern World Ventures, for example, don't display their postal address prominently on their web site. Others hide their phone numbers—some software companies are particularly bad about this—to keep their staff from becoming overloaded with inquiries.

We welcome updates and corrections by suppliers or readers, if you find errors or think the directory omits significant resources. We have not tried to be exhaustive, but rather, the goal has been to provide easy access to products and services mentioned in the book. For update, corrections, and additions, please send email to *errors@q3press.com* or phone 877 Q3P-0500 (877 737-0500).

Aerostich
8 South 18th Avenue West
Duluth, MN 55806
800 222-1994
www.aerostich.com

American Motorcyclist Association
13515 Yarmouth Drive
Pickerington, OH 43147
614 856-1900
www.ama-cycle.org

American Supercamp
553 Lakewood Court
Windsor, CO 80550
970 674-9434
www.americansupercamp.com

Baja Designs Incorporated
185 Bosstick Road
San Marcos, CA 92069
760 560-BAJA (560-2252)
www.bajadesigns.com

California Superbike School
940 San Fernando Road
Los Angeles, CA 90065
323 224-2734
www.californiasuperbikeschool.com

Cruz Tools
13645 Tuolumne Road
Sonora, CA 95370
888 909-8665
www.cruztools.com

CycoActive Products
701 34th Avenue
Seattle, WA 98122
800 491-CYCO (491-2926)
www.cycoactive.com

Danny Walker
(See American Supercamp)

DeLorme
Two DeLorme Drive
P.O. Box 298
Yarmouth, ME 04096
800 561-5105
www.delorme.com

DowCo
4230 Clipper Drive
Manitowoc, WI 54220
www.dowco-inc.com/mcycles.html

E-Z Leaker
P.O. Box 6406
Metairie, LA 70009
888 704-0033
www.ezleaker.com

Fog City
Modern World Ventures
P.O. Box 16010
Oakland, CA 94610
800 436-4248
www.modernworld.com/fogcity/fogcity.html

GPS City
6 Sunset Way, Suite 108
Henderson, NV 89014
866 GPS CITY (477-2489)
www.gpscity.com

Harley-Davidson of Greenville
455 Congaree Road
Greenville, SC 29607
864 234-1340
www.h-dog.com

Harley Owners Group
P.O. Box 453
Milwaukee, WI 53201
800 CLUB HOG (258-2464)
www.hog.com

Harley Transport (see Motorcycle Shipping)

Hornet Deer Whistles
P.O. Box 790
Aurora, OH 44202
800 475-3563
www.xp3hornet.com

Iron Butt Association
6326 W. Grace Street
Chicago, IL 60634
www.ironbutt.com

Lazy Rider Company
3707 66th Street
Lubbock, TX 79413
800 687-7806
www.lazyrider.com

Michael's Harley Davidson
7601 Redwood Drive
Cotati, CA 94931
800 400-2011
www.michaelsharleydavidson.com

Motorcycle Safety Foundation
2 Jenner Street, Suite 150
Irvine, CA 92618
949 727-3227
www.msf-usa.org

Motorcycle Shipping
866 798-0805
www.motorcycleshipping.com
www.harleytransport.com

Performance Bike
One Performance Way
Chapel Hill, NC 27514
919 933-9113
www.performancebike.com

PIAA Corporation, USA
15370 SW Millikan Way
Beaverton, OR 97006
503 643-7422
www.piaa.com

RM Racing
15651 North 83rd Way, #2
Scottsdale, AZ 85260
480 483-2444
www.rmhid.com

Road America
3081 Salzedo Street
Coral Gables, FL 33134
888 443-5896
www.road-america.com

Road Runner Sports
5549 Copley Drive
San Diego, CA 92111
800 636-3560
www.roadrunnersports.com

SAC Motorcycle Luggage
2180 Elmwood Avenue
Buffalo, NY 14216
800 445-8946
www.coolsac.com

Schampa All Weather Products
P.O. Box 6145
Chandler, AZ 85246
877 440-6458
www.schampa.com

Street Wizard
Adept Computer Solutions
10951 Sorrento Valley Road,
Suite 1G
San Diego, CA 92121
858 597-1772
www.streetwizard.com

Throttle Rocker Motorcycle Accessories
P.O. Box 66198
Scotts Valley, CA 95067
800 757-2453
www.throttlerocker.com

Whitehorse Press
P.O. Box 60
North Conway, NH 03860
800 531-1133
www.whitehorsepress.com

Appendix D:

Motorcycle Safety Information

What's the truth about motorcycle safety? You may need to convince a spouse or friend that your trip isn't among the worst ideas on earth. Here are the facts. The source of this data is a 45-page report prepared by the Mathematical Analysis Division of the National Center for Statistics and Analysis, part of the National Highway Traffic Safety Administration (NHTSA), within the U.S. Department of Transportation (DOT).[1] If that's not sufficiently impressive, then probably your spouse, friend, or family member is not going to accept what you say anyway.

So, here's how you can protect yourself and *try* to reassure them. Many of these statistics have remained remarkably constant over the years, so we need to *know* what causes accidents.[2] Each

---

[1] U.S. Department of Transportation, National Highway Traffic Safety Administration. Fatal Single Vehicle Motorcycle Crashes. Report # DOT HS 809 360. Washington, DC. October 2001. For the report, see *http://www-nrd.nhtsa.dot.gov/pdf/nrd-30/NCSA/Rpts/2001/809-360.pdf*

[2] Mathematically, however, note that you cannot just add percentages—because the categories overlap. For example, you cannot say, "Well, 33% of the fatally injured riders didn't have a motorcycle license and 50% didn't have on a helmet, so I will eliminate 83% of the risk if I have a valid motorcycle license and wear a helmet."

of the categories listed here also points to a *significant* way to reduce your risk when riding.

- First, you should know that *single vehicle* motorcycle fatalities (SVMF) constitute almost half of motorcycle deaths—ranging from 43% to 47% depending on the year, over the past 10 years. We worry about intersections and other motorists—and rightly so. But about half the time, if we crash, we do it to ourselves. This is why "Riding Techniques" have been emphasized throughout this book.

- Almost 33% of riders involved in a SVMF (that is, we did it to ourselves) *did not even have a proper license*. If you have a valid license to ride a motorcycle—much less have had training from the Motorcycle Safety Foundation, Danny Walker's American Supercamp, or one of the other fine racing courses—then your chances improve by at least one-third. Pilots are constantly in training. It's not a bad idea for motorcyclists, too.

- More than 50% of fatally injured motorcyclists in SVMF were *not wearing a helmet*. Don't be a hard head on this one. Wear a helmet for your long trip. If that statistic weren't sufficiently grim, a separate study since helmet laws were repealed in Arkansas and Texas shows that motorcycle deaths rates rose 21% and 31%, respectively, in those states during the first full year after repeal. I love riding without a helmet as much as anyone, but it's a risk I'm no longer prepared to take out of consideration for those who love me.

- About 50% of SVMF occur while *negotiating a curve* prior to the crash. So, watch your corner entry speed—especially when you are on secondary (non-interstate freeway type roads). One other conclusion noted in the study is that more motorcycle fatalities are occurring on rural roads. Does this suggest illegal racing? Maybe so, maybe not. But watch yourself in the curves and along rural roads.

- A full 75% of SVMF occur on undivided roadways. And remember, these are single vehicle crashes—so this is not attributable to the dreaded "someone turned left in front of me." Despite the higher speeds on divided highways, they're safer. Add a median with barrier, and the statistics show only 9% of SVMF occur on such roads. Obviously, this doesn't mean that you should never ride the back roads that many of us enjoy so much. What it does mean is (1) when you are on an undivided roadway, be especially alert, and (2) if you really need to be somewhere soon, find a suitable highway.

- In almost 60% of SVMF, *speeding* was a contributing factor. I know that it's fun to ride fast, but draw your own conclusions here and set your risk reduction strategy accordingly.

- A staggering 42% of SVMF involved a blood *alcohol* level greater than 0.10.[3] We can avoid this by limiting our alcohol consumption before getting on our bikes, or waiting to ride if we have had a few drinks (see the next point, also). But sadly, 47% of SVMF involved operators whose blood alcohol tested 0.00—that is, riders who were completely sober. This fact means we must know techniques and exercise judgment to protect ourselves from ourselves.

- Almost 60% of the SVMF occur *at night*. This statistic requires further analysis, since we might wonder whether

---

[3] The standard measure is grams per deciliter (g/dl). In most states in the U.S., persons with a blood alcohol level of higher 0.08 g/dl are considered to be intoxicated.

this is the result of riders over-riding their headlight at night or fatigue—or does the statistic relate to having a few beers after stopping off at a pub? Thankfully, the NHTSA did the analysis for us. The results show that fatal accidents at night involve alcohol three times as often as accidents during the day. A full 75% of nighttime SMVF involve alcohol. Stay away from alcohol or allow one hour from bottle to throttle for each drink. Remember that a beer, a glass of wine, or a cocktail mixed in normal proportions all contain about the same amount of alcohol.

- A full 82% percent of SVMF occur when the bike *left the roadway* and 60% of SVMF result from a collision with a fixed object. At first glance, these statistics seem to be one of those "Well, duh!" conclusions. It's logical that most SVMF will take place after the bike leaves the road and when it hits something. But the longer I thought about these statistics, the clearer it became they actually make two important points:

First, if you can use good technique to keep the bike on the road—even if you have to lay it down—your chances of surviving the crash are higher. However, make no mistake; deliberately laying a bike down is a crash. You haven't avoided crashing; you've just attempted to minimize personal injury. A better approach would be to learn a technique akin to Danny Walker's "push it down, push it farther down" that actually allows you to negotiate your way through a dangerous situation.

Second, even if it is absolutely clear you are going to crash—but if you have any control at all—ride the bike all the way to the crash site. I don't mean just stay on the bike. I mean, insofar as you can, choose where you want to crash. This might seem obvious. But evidence from flight training suggests that inexperienced pilots, faced with an inevitable crash, sometimes give up *when options exist to reduce the severity of the crash*. If you must crash, do it on your terms. So, ride the bike, ride the bike, ride your bike! Pick the softest place to crash. Pick an open place. Deliberately lay it down. Sacrifice the bike but save yourself. Let's hope that through good technique and defensive riding you never have to make this kind of choice. But don't ever stop fighting for the best outcome until the bike has stopped moving.

OK, what about the other 50% of fatal motorcycle accidents— the ones that involve other vehicles? NHTSA studies are remarkable for the absence of data about multiple vehicle crashes. Perhaps part of the reason is because authorities feel a greater effort needs to be made to spread the safety messages to motorcyclists about their risks in single vehicle crashes. And, that is true. If we are totally in control of approximately 50% of the fatal motorcycle accidents, then let's pay more attention to the contributing factors.

But that still begs the question, "What can we do to reduce our risk of colliding with another vehicle and being injured or killed?" Unfortunately, most advice is anecdotal, based on experience rather than statistical analysis. On that basis, however, remember the following pointers as you ride.

Watch intersections like a hawk!
At any given intersection, there are at least three hazards:

- Intersecting traffic that does not stop.
- Traffic that turns left in front of you.
- Traffic flowing around you that does something unexpected.

Ways to minimize the *single-threat* scenarios are obvious. Always look for traffic that does not stop, regardless of who has the right of way. Be extraordinarily careful about someone choosing to turn left in front of you, even when it's clear that they cannot do so without endangering you. Scan constantly to maintain situational awareness about who or what is behind *and* beside you, when approaching an intersection. You may need to stop rapidly to avoid an unsafe left turn ahead of you— but avoiding the car making the left turn will be little consolation if you are rear-ended or swerve into a vehicle beside you.

The variety of *multiple-threat* combinations is too high to systematically discuss. But try to imagine some of these scenarios next time you are sitting in an intersection. For example, imagine you're sitting in the left turn lane, waiting for traffic to clear. Suddenly, in your mirror, you see a driver approaching from behind at a speed that makes it clear he or she doesn't see you. The flow of traffic is solid to your left and to your right. Where do you go?

Chances are the only open space in the intersection is directly *ahead* of you—in the left turn lane that faces you on the opposite side of the intersection. We don't think about using that space under normal traffic rules, because it's off limits to us. But faced with a certain rear-ender, would you rather sit where you are or ride straight across the intersection and try to hide among the cars opposite you that are also waiting to turn left? I know what I'd do!

Be prickly

This technique was mentioned earlier in the book. Do whatever it takes to make yourself and your bike visible.

Recent research summarized in many motorcycle publications suggests that *drivers see only what they expect to see*. That statement is important enough to bear repeating: research shows *drivers see only what they expect to see*. So, even if you are clearly in their field of vision—but they are looking for other *cars*—you are invisible.

Ride with your lights on, mount an American flag on your bike, use hand signals, zig-zag within the confines of your lane, rev your engine, honk your horn (just don't depend on your horn, since most stock motorcycle horns aren't of much use). But never, under any circumstances, assume that other motorists see you. Just today, as I was returning home from lunch, a driver in an SUV pulled out of a shopping center directly in front of me. But the situation was never life threatening, because that's *exactly what I expected to happen.*

Control the things that minimize the risk of a SVMF
Do this and you'll also go a long way toward ensuring your safety in a multiple vehicle accident. Have a valid license; get training; wear a helmet; be especially careful about undivided roadways; watch your speed; stay away from alcohol when riding; and, when all else fails, choose how and where you want to crash—rather than allowing another motorist to choose for you.

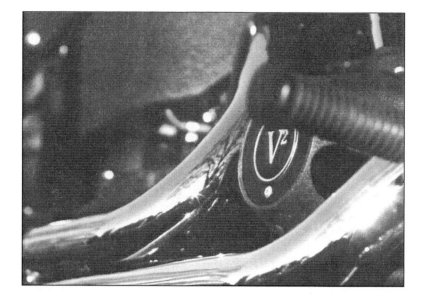

Bibliography

Alvord, Katie. *Divorce Your Car*. Gabriola Island, BC: New Society Publishers, 2000.

Ayres, Ron. *Against the Wind: A Rider's Account of the Incredible Iron Butt Rally*. North Conway, NH: Whitehorse Press, 1997.

Ayres, Ron. *Against the Clock: The Incredible Story of the 7/49*. North Conway, NH: Whitehorse Press, 1999.

Barr, Dave. *Riding the Edge*. Bodfish, CA: Dave Barr Publications, 1999.

Bartell, Allen J. *Alaskan Aberration*. Trinity, TX: Flat Black Publishing, 1997.

Bausenhart, Werner. *8 Around the Americas on a Motorcycle*. Brooklyn, NY: Legas, 2000.

Bleys, Rose. "Sutter CEO in SR to Step Down." *The Press Democrat*. April 20, 2002.

California State Automobile Association home page. 1996-2002. 29 August 2002. <*www.csaa.com*>

Campbell, Joseph. *The Hero with a Thousand Faces*. 2nd ed. Princeton: Princeton University Press, 1968.

Carlin, Ben. *Half Safe: Across the Atlantic by Jeep*. London: André Deutsch Limited, 1955.

Carlin, Ben. *The Other Half of Half Safe*. Guilford, Western Australia: Guilford Grammar School Foundation, Inc., 1989.

Chicago Marathon home page. 2002. 29 August 2002. <*www.chicagomarathon.com*>

Code, Keith. *A Twist of the Wrist*. Glendale, CA: Code Break, 1997.

CycoActive Products. *CycoActive Garmin GPS Comparison Chart*. 2002. 29 August 2002. <*www.cycoactive.com/gps/gps_compare.html*>

De Mente, Boyé Lafayette. *Once a Fool: From Japan to Alaska by Amphibious Jeep*. <*www.hadami.com/bookinfo/details.asp?bookID=114*>

Dominguez, Joe and Vicki Robin. *Your Money or Your Life*. New York: Penguin Books, 1992.

Drakulic, Slavenka. *How We Survived Communism and Even Laughed*. New York: Harper Collins, 1991.

Eliot, T.S. "The Love Song of J. Alfred Prufrock." *Collected Poems: 1909-1962*. Orlando, FL: Harcourt Brace & Company, 1963, 1991.

eBay home page. August 2002. 29 August 2002. <*www.ebay.com*>

Fromkin, David. *A Peace to End All Peace*. New York: Avon Books, 1989.

Galloway, Jeff. Marathon: You Can Do It. Bolinas, CA: Shelter Publications, 2001.

Gann, Ernest. *Song of the Sirens*. New York: Simon and Schuster, 1968.

Gleick, James. *Chaos: Making a New Science*. New York: Viking Penguin, Inc., 1987.

Google home page. 2002. 29 August 2002. *<www.google.com>*

Grahame, Kenneth. *Wind in the Willows*. New York: Aladdin Books, 1989.

Henry's R1100GS LED tailight backup page. 2002. 29 August 2002. *<www.xs4all.nl/~hkuijer/taillight.htm>*

Herring, Hebert B. "Scouting for Work, but Close to the Nest." *The New York Times*. April 28, 2002.

Horwood, William. *The Willows in Winter*. New York: St. Martin's Press, 1994.

Horwood, William. *Toad Triumphant*. New York: St. Martin's Press, 1998.

MapQuest home page. 2002. 29 August 2002. *<www.mapquest.com>*

Masi, C.G. *How to Set Up Your Motorcycle Workshop*. North Conway, NH: Whitehorse Press, 1996.

Mehaffey, Joe, and Jack Yaezel. *Joe Mehaffey and Jack Yaezel's GPS Information Website* home page. 2002. 29 August 2002. *<www.joe.mehaffey.com>*

Mehaffey, Joe, and Jack Yaezel. *Low Cost GPS and Moving Map PC Software Reviews* page. Revised 5 June, 2002. 29 August 2002. *<www.joe.mehaffey.com/ot-20.htm>*

Miller, William Ian. *The Mystery of Courage*. Cambridge, MA: Harvard University Press, 2000.

Road Tests / Product Tests page. Motorsports Network. 1997-2002. February 2002. *<www.motorsports-network.com/prodtest.HTM>*

Pedersen, Helge. *10 Years on 2 Wheels*. Seattle: Elfin Cove Press, 1998.

Pieper, Josef. *Leisure: The Basis of Culture*. South Bend, IN: St. Augustine's Press, Inc., 1998.

Runner's World. Emmaus, PA. *<www.runnersworld.com>*

Salvadori, Clement. "On Touring: Overcoming Inertia." *Rider,* August 2001, p. 28.

Salvadori, Clement. "Mental Lollygagging." *Rider*, February 2002, pp. 20-21.

Sears, Barry. *The Zone*. New York: HarperCollins, 1995.

Simoni, Wayne "Trees." Email message to the author. 26 January, 2002.

Thomas, Dylan. "Do Not Go Gentle into that Good Night." *The Academy of American Poets* web site. 1997-2002. 29 August 2002. *<www.poets.org/poems/poems.cfm?prmID=1159>*

U.S. Department of Transportation, National Highway Traffic Safety Administration, "Fatal Single Vehicle Motorcycle Crashes." Report # DOT HS 809 360 *<www-nrd.nhtsa.dot.gov/pdf/nrd-30/NCSA/Rpts/2001/809-360.pdf227>*

Wilderness Survival home page. 2001-2002. 29 August 2002. *<www.wilderness-survival.net>*

Yahoo Maps page. 2002. 29 August 2002. *<maps.yahoo.com>*

Zuboff, Shoshanna. *In the Age of the Smart Machine: The Future of Work and Power*. New York: Basic Books, Inc., 1988.

Index

About the Author

Dick Peck attended a Harley Owners Group rally in 1999, which rekindled his passion for motorcycling. Within two weeks, he purchased a black Harley Softail that his wife, Susan, promptly named "Eli." With Eli, they have traveled the California coast, Lake Tahoe, and the Sierra Nevada. Before reprioritizing his life, Dick held senior management positions in publishing, market research, and international business. He was part of a team that developed one of the first Internet portals and, much earlier, he enjoyed a stint as a jazz musician. He and Susan live in Santa Rosa, California, with their collie/husky mix, Dudley. *Crossing America* is Dick's third book, following two works published while in the music industry.

In addition to motorcycling, Dick enjoys running, bicycling and the company of family and friends. A native of the South, he holds an MBA from the University of South Carolina and a BA in English from the University of Kentucky. Dick and Susan have been residents of California since 1991.

About Q3 Press

Q3 Press was formed to help make deferred dreams real. In a too-busy world, many life ambitions are postponed until we realize, "If not now, when?"

Q3's *You Can*™ series focuses on dreams achieved—learning to fly, making ocean passages, traveling long distances by motorcycle, running marathons and ultra-events, and bicycling cross-country. Each book offers detailed how-to's set in a narrative journal that chronicles the writer's triumph, as well as the challenges overcome along the way.

Formed by four publishing veterans, with experience from McGraw-Hill to Miller Freeman, as well as online startups, Q3 has its headquarters in Santa Rosa, CA, the heart of Sonoma wine country and the home of the new Charles M. Schulz Museum.

Photo Credits

Q3 Press and the author acknowledge and thank the following people for providing photographs for the book.

Joy F. Peck, *p. 18, p. 119, p. 200.*
Robert R. Peck, *Cover photo, p. 69, p. 206, p. 228.*
Susan B. Peck, *Back cover photo, p. 150.*
All other photos courtesy of the author.

Bob Peck, cover photo shoot